Who Told You You Were Naked?

WHO TOLD YOU

YU

WERE

Naked?

Overcoming Mental Illness,
Dismantling Tormenting Demons,
Unveiling Your True Identity

ELIZABETH
CLEMENTS

NASHVILLE

NEW YORK • LONDON • MELBOURNE • VANCOUVER

Who Told You You Were Naked?

Overcoming Mental Illness, Dismantling Tormenting Demons, Unveiling Your True Identity

Published in New York, New York, by Morgan James Publishing. Morgan James is a trademark of Morgan James, LLC. www.MorganJamesPublishing.com

Proudly distributed by Publishers Group West®

Morgan James BOGO™

A **FREE** ebook edition is available for you or a friend with the purchase of this print book.

CLEARLY SIGN YOUR NAME ABOVE

Instructions to claim your free ebook edition:
1. Visit MorganJamesBOGO.com
2. Sign your name CLEARLY in the space above
3. Complete the form and submit a photo of this entire page
4. You or your friend can download the ebook to your preferred device

ISBN 9781636982304 paperback
ISBN 9781636982311 ebook
Library of Congress Control Number: 2023938908

Cover Design by:
Rachel Lopez
www.r2cdesign.com

Interior Design by:
Christopher Kirk
www.GFSstudio.com

Morgan James PUBLISHING
Builds
with...
Habitat for Humanity Peninsula and Greater Williamsburg

Morgan James is a proud partner of Habitat for Humanity Peninsula and Greater Williamsburg. Partners in building since 2006.

Get involved today! Visit: www.morgan-james-publishing.com/giving-back

I dedicate this book to the many influential people that made my healing journey possible. To my mother and father, thank you for giving me grace during my darkest of days, for continually lifting me in prayer and believing I could have a different future in Christ. To my husband Bill, who has walked with me hand in hand through ominous trenches in overcoming trauma and refused to leave, for calling forth the gold behind the girl that didn't know how to shine, thank you for constantly stoking my fire, propelling me forward into the destiny God designed.

To my previous bosses, Sheila and Jennifer, thank you for taking a stand for Christ and showing me the way to Jesus.

To my inner healing therapist, Anj, you showed me what it means to be born again and assisted me in defining that inward reality. To Roddie, Mama Hottie, on fire for the Lord and who baptized me in the Holy Ghost and fire, your contagious fire allowed me to catch the embers of your flame and ignite a passion and love for Jesus, too; you taught me how to stand in the Lord through His Word and war from scripture. Your crown is filled with the most precious jewels. To the friends that didn't leave my side as I walked through the crossfires of hell overcoming the enemy in my life, thank you for your love, prayers and support. To all of my lovely clients who have witnessed this journey, prayed and supported me through it all, your love has been a precious stone in rebuilding this new life.

TABLE OF CONTENTS

Introductory Prayer

Father God, I thank you for your amazing grace, your reckless love, your mercy that advocates for the sinner. For your strong arm that reaches low to raise up the dead to triumphantly live again in Jesus. I thank you that we are never too far gone if we are still allowed to breathe your air on this earth. I declare you are God and there is no one like you. No created being on earth could ever usurp you and your great power. I declare you, Jesus, as the one, true, living God. Father, thank you for sending your son Jesus to live a sinless life, bear our burdens, our weakness, our infirmities, our transgressions and sin and overcome our shame, condemnation and sorrows on the cross.

Jesus, you know what it feels like to have fleshly limitations, to have weaknesses in our frames. You, Jesus, were tested and tempted in every way like we are but still you remained radi-

cally obedient to the Father, even to death on the cross so that we could have life and live abundantly and eternally with you. We bestow on you all praise, honor and glory. You deserve all our highest praise. Thank you, Jesus, that you are now interceding on our behalf, as our advocate to the Father, that we may have all power to overcome the darkness in our lives. Thank you for fighting for us even now to overcome death and spiritual separation so that we can experience a life of intimacy without shame before you and with you. Thank you for your intercession to help make us in your likeness in true righteousness and holiness. You continually lead our lives out of darkness into the light and transform us from glory to glory as you open our eyes to new life and how to live abundantly in you. Help us see the blessings, glory, and favor you bestow upon us daily. Help us recognize your hand working in our lives so we can manifest the things that you have assigned for us to co-labor and glorify your holy name in. Help us to be good stewards of your grace because we know it is by grace and grace alone that we live, move, and have our being. Thank you for your Word, your powerful working Word that sustains by your breath and for your love which rests upon us through your presence. We give this time and space right now for you to speak to us, heal us, and anoint us. Come reside in us and fill us with your love, joy, and peace. We confess your kingdom is all we want, all we seek. Fill us with the abundance of life and joy in your presence. We love and praise your holy name, Jesus. Amen!

I pray that every eye, every heart sitting under the influence of your Word will be radically transformed from death to life by the power of the Holy Spirit that has the ability to cut through the soul and spirit and raise the dead to life. May God use this testimony to transform and resurrect souls to the advancement of the end time army for the Kingdom of God. In the name of Yeshua! Amen!

INTRODUCTION

T hroughout my tenure as a professional hairstylist, I
have had the pleasure of working with hundreds of
individuals. Most have allowed me to take a unique
glimpse into the deep waters of their lives. I feel honored
when clients trust me with their innermost, intimate, personal
struggles. When I first began my career, I was surprised to
find people were so willing to engage in serious conversation
with me. I felt unequipped for and challenged by bearing their
burdens along with my own, but I wanted to for the heartfelt
compassion for their struggles.

As I plowed into my new career, I simultaneously began
my own journey of inner healing with the Lord. As healing
began to break forth in my life, I found joy in helping clients
who shared some of the same issues—anxiety, depression, sui-

cidal ideation, addiction and divorce, to name a few. The full spectrum of people—young and old, men and women alike, varying socioeconomic status have all been affected by the ever-changing climate of our culture. I've yet to speak with a person that hasn't reached for an anchor of hope and comfort in challenging times. This paradigm has propelled me deeper into the Word of God to help them find wisdom, revelation and understanding to help in times of need. Even if I do not directly quote scripture, I always share revelation from the Word because I know it is a seed that, when sown, will not return void but accomplish the purposes of God for healing and deliverance in that person's life.

In 2020 during the height of the Covid pandemic, the Lord opened a door for me to begin my own salon to further my ministry in a private setting. I named it "Hairapy" because many clients look to me not only for hair advice but for therapy as well. Through their encouragement and the Holy Spirit's conviction, I've written this book detailing my journey—its process, the pain, the tears—in hopes of helping many others discover their own breakthroughs and the outcome of a surrendered life to Jesus.

I tell you the truth, unless a kernel of wheat is planted in the soil and dies, it remains alone. But its death will produce many new kernels—a plentiful harvest of new lives.
(John 12:24, NLT)

PART ONE

Note to the Reader:

In Part One of *Who Told You You Were Naked*, I share the story of who I was before the Lord changed my life. My story is not an easy one to take in, but I share an honest account of my history. I share my story because I want others to know that the truth is not something to hide or be ashamed of. I have found that confession and honesty with myself and others has led to health and healing I longed to receive.

I write not with eloquent words or penmanship, I come with the testimony of the wonder-working power of Jesus and His Holy Spirit. I come to share my life transformed by the power of the gospel of Jesus Christ. To some, I will be a pleasing fragrance of breakthrough and deliverance, to others, a stench of conviction. "For we are to God the sweet aroma of Christ among those who are being saved and those who are perishing. To the one, we are an odor of death and demise; to the other, a fragrance that brings life" (2 Corinthians 2:15–16a BSB). Either way, I pray the Holy Spirit breathes through this work and that dry bones begin to shake and come to life. I pray the truths presented from the gospel and the testimony of its power in my life will work deeply and richly in your inner being so that your life, too, can be transformed by the only person that can redeem life from the grave, the only one worthy of all honor, glory and praise, King JESUS!

Chapter 1—

AN INTERNAL DISRUPTION

Then I passed by and saw you wallowing in your blood, and as you lay there in your blood I said to you, "Live!" There I said to you "Live!" (Ezekiel 16:6, BSB)

In the middle of the COVID-19 crisis, the alarm struck midnight in my spirit: it was time. For years, I'd felt a crescendo building up of something that would come change and catapult society into a "new normal." I did not know it would be a plague, but in the way culture and society functioned, it felt like we were on an unstoppable steam train that needed a reset. Now was that time, but what would be the outcome? After the shifting and shaking, how would society emerge? What would our world look like? While stationed at home with a moment to catch my breath as my mother was keeping my little thirteen-month-old, I sat and pondered the parallels of the pandemic to the one the Lord had just led me through.

I picked up a book, and the first lines I read were these: "Books are supposed to be imperfect, if not it allows every-thing to be summed up, tied up in a nice little bow with nothing left to mystery." Knowing I had a little gem on my computer waiting to be completed, the sentiment panged my heart. Somehow, I had allowed fear of failure to instigate itself in me, and I'd been paralyzed and made excuses from making forward progress to complete the book the Lord had commis-sioned me to write years earlier. I reminded myself that I was no longer a slave to fear. I thoughtfully grabbed that lie captive and took it into the light of God's truth. I reminded myself that the Holy Spirit of the Lord leads me into triumph, not failure. I disengaged from the deception of the enemy and battled for-ward to what I knew lost souls needed, which was a testimony of the Lord's goodness, His mercy and faithfulness to a once sinner, now saint like me.

I sat and asked God, What do you want me to do?

He said, "Write what's on your heart. Share with others what you've learned from me, 'for my yoke is easy and my burden is light' (Matthew 11:30, NIV). It won't be perfect, and it doesn't have to be because where I have taken you through wilderness, through the sea, up and back down a mountain or two, through tough terrain and refreshing waters has all been marked by imperfect progress but progress none the less."

I will lead the blind by ways they have not known,
along unfamiliar paths I will guide them;
I will turn the darkness into light before them
and make the rough places smooth.
These are the things I will do;
I will not forsake them.
(Isaiah 42:16, NIV)

What I observed during the worldwide epidemic was a widespread yearning for a foundational truth and hope, something real and steady upon which to rest in comfort through the wind and stand in the waves of change. Now it feels to me the harvest is ripe and ready for the truth, ready for something of substance to lay a firm foundation upon. The heart's cry for rest from weariness and for joy instead of constant mourning is a theme. I observed during the crisis that much of what carried pleasure, fulfillment and promise became dashed dreams. Many enterprising people who started businesses closed their doors; many workers at the same job forever lost their positions or were furloughed. Kids who thought school was the most dreadful thing found themselves lost in a sea of at-home education. And now they have a hard time getting back in the swing of school-based curriculum. Everything we knew was getting knocked to smithereens. The Word says that whatever can be shaken will, and now more than ever, that truth is evident (Hebrews 12:27).

If the crisis wasn't bad enough in the way it threatened lives and shut down the economy, the world at large continued to experience other tragedies, too. Locusts in Africa, tornados across the Midwest, record snowfall followed by wildfires in the Western states—insult added to injury everywhere. What is there to hope in? What is there to anchor life to when everything is being stripped bare and laid waste?

In many ways, the situation in the world at large seemed to closely parallel the chastening that had occurred in my life over the past decade. Worldly pleasures, social outlets, sources of identity and idols: God beckoned me to lay them all down on an altar to be burned by the consuming love of Jesus. It was not what I wanted to happen, but deep down I knew it needed to happen. It needed to happen because the way I had been functioning wasn't working. Internal lies led to my beliefs, they left me hollow and dry. I believed if I could get out of my small town and make something big of myself, I would somehow feel a transfer of power, and magically, the anxiety and depression that crippled my personality would fade into the background. I believed that with enough money, I could outrun the daily mental turmoil I lived in. I believed drinking would numb my pain and eventually eliminate it altogether and that cigarettes sufficiently alleviated my anxiety. I believed that if men thought I was attractive, that would make me strong, and their attention would make me important. I believed that shopping at high-end stores made me cosmopolitan and that eating expensive foods made me more sophisticated.

I thought Jesus was stupid. If I didn't choose to be born, why on earth should I believe in Him? I thought His sacrifice was irrelevant and that Christians were a weird bunch of hypocrites who dressed up on Sundays in suits and dresses and ate potato salad and turkey sandwiches after church. How would doing what they do make me better? If their religion had the power it claimed, then why did I feel so much pain? I'd been in religion as a child. So why was I hurting? However, none of what I presumed would be fulfilling was working, either, and I was in the worst hole of my life. I sheepishly admitted that acknowledging my need for Jesus might be the way.

I had come to the end of myself. In desperation, I cried out, "Your will, not mine Lord—I need you." I knew from childhood that calling upon the Lord in hard times was something to do, but this time was different. I actually wanted a change. But what would this change involve? This time, praying was scary. Scary because I knew things I had relied upon as sources of comfort, pleasure and identity might be taken away. What would be left? How would that look? What if I lost everything?

However, what little I had to keep me satisfied was also wearing me dry. My sources of comfort and temporal happiness were ever-changing and inadequate in keeping me content. Internally, I knew any peace I thought I felt was an illusion. I knew something had to change. Deep down, I knew it wasn't my circumstances—it was me. How could I change? I had been the same forever, and even though I'd tried to change, and could for a brief time, I would go back to similar routines of self-destructive behaviors. What I needed was a heart transplant, not mere behavior modification.

My life had come to a diverging point. Was I going to continue down the road of consumption—food, alcohol, cigarettes, men, clothing, shoes, purses? Or was I going to lay all that to the side to figure out why I ached inside? What made me keep going back to things of no use and no value that were slowly bringing death to my soul? I had to figure out what was going on so I could experience peace in my life, feel alive and find purpose and meaning. Why did life seem to offer pleasure but in the end, it left me feeling nothing, with no meaning?

It was a dry, parched existence. I liken it to when you get super thirsty in the summer, and your mouth gets dry and sticky. It's that kind of thirst when you want something real. I wanted that need satisfied. I wanted to be filled and not be left with a "needing more" hangover.

> **Day and night your hand of discipline was heavy on me.**
> **My strength evaporated like water in the summer heat. (Psalm 32:4, NLT)**

I awoke daily, feeling the need to dull the interior ache of anxiety and hopelessness. I searched for something to help me feel joy and peace I had yet to experience. I desperately sought solace beyond the unconventional methods I had already tried: cutting away (literally), drowning away (alcohol), breathing away (smoking), or having sex (to fill me up with something I knew could give me inward pleasure—but it was fleeting, and the moment was soon over).

My now-husband would say, "Elizabeth, you can't solve your problems by creating new ones," and he was right. I was either desperately trying to feel something or nothing at all.

Something was missing, something deep inside I couldn't put a finger on. I was lost, heavily burdened, with pain from an identity so confused—I was a mess.

For years, I sought to quell the emotional roller coaster that existed in me. I didn't know how it ended up there. I had some fairly good assumptions but no hard truths as to why I had ended up smoked out, drunk out, almost dead from an eating disorder and questions as to why I couldn't seem to function in a relationship with the opposite sex or the same sex (yes, I tried that, too). I wanted to be different, but I had tried and failed miserably. I would make declarations at the beginning of my day: "I will...," but the night would come, and I was still the same, popping bottles and lighting a cigarette, losing my temper, saying things I later regretted or breaking something in rage because I couldn't control the anger that simmered like hot molten lava in my chest.

You're too much. You're not enough. Not capable. Irresponsible. You're not safe. Victim. Shame. Insecure. Weak. Confused. Abandoned. Rejected.

These lies kept manifesting in my thoughts. I tried to find answers to help heal the uncomfortable shame and rejection I felt deep inside. I needed an explanation to understand my feelings, but the answers never led to deliverance. Instead, the same lies—that I wasn't good enough, was a reject, and something was really wrong with me—circulated in my mind like a boasting, never-ending, relentless chatter.

Doctors diagnosed me with bipolar disorder, borderline personality disorder (BPD), anxiety and depression. The labels made me feel like I was worth no more than reduced-priced cans in a grocery store, the ones usually found piled high in a buggy somewhere in the center of the store. The ones that have been beaten up and banged around in shipping or by a customer mishandling them. Usually displayed in a disorderly, jumbled fashion, these less-than-perfect containers are often overlooked and only noticed if someone wants a discounted price. That was how I felt: cheap, discounted, and forgotten.

Yes, that was me. I had made decisions to feel used and abused, less than what I was worth. I made decisions based on the voices that kept me on the run. Because of these internal, shameful messages, I had dug myself into a pit of despair, hopelessness, and grief. Sin in my life created a snowball of errors I didn't know how to begin to work my way out of. My life was constructed around lies and hiding. I didn't want anyone to find out who I was because if they knew the real me, I would be exposed as the faker I knew myself to be, even though I put up a good front.

I had learned to stop the inner voice of correction that would have brought me to the light again. For some reason, I was drawn to darkness. I found it intriguing. When you keep silencing the voice that says, *"Stop, don't do that,"* you slowly sear your conscience. For me, that voice would come and go. *"I wouldn't be so sure of that person. Watch out: he is flattering you to get what he wants out of you."* The more I got into my troubled behavior, the voice about what I should do grew silent. Over it, the voice of my flesh cried out, *"Do it, have more of it! You need more of it.*" I once told a friend, "If you were inside my mind, you wouldn't be friends with me."

The voices of shame had an ear-piercing scream. Paranoia set in: *"If people knew you, Elizabeth, they wouldn't like you. If you let your guard down, people will know how dirty and nasty you really are."* This internal monologue was nonstop. I wanted to silence it but couldn't make the voices stop, and what I attracted in friendships and partners were extensions of them. *"You aren't worthy. You are trash."* I spent years in toxic relationships that only confirmed what these voices made me believe: I wasn't good enough and therefore deserved this kind of treatment.

I was coming to the end of myself as my life kept unraveling with bad choice after bad choice. I desperately wanted to be known so I could somehow be put back together, but the thought of intimacy was terrifying.

However, at this point I didn't care how much pain it would cause me to re-live the heartache of my past; I just knew I needed new life pouring into me, a fresh start. I was tired of putting up a facade of standardized beauty to cover my pain. I knew how to dress up the outside and appear put-together. I even won best dressed in high school—imagine that! However, all the makeup I wore, clothes I put on, hair and nails I did to mimic what I saw on the covers of fashion magazines could no longer mask my inner turmoil. Inside, I was an insecure ball of nerves and a people-pleaser trying to fit in no matter the cost. I did whatever it took to fit in and appear to be in the inside group—drinking, smoking, going to parties, and sleeping with numerous guys. I did it all, and the more I sold out to this image, the more it empowered the lies within me.

I was frustrated by my endless search for answers—as if the world could ever give me some sort of handbook of reasoning and resolution for what happened and explain how to move forward. I exhausted the lists of the world's ways of seeking help. I had a counselor for dialectical behavioral therapy (DBT), a counselor for cognitive behavioral therapy (CBT), psychotherapist after psychotherapist, script for this, a script for that. (Let me note: there is a time and space for prescription medication for anxiety and depression.) I spent many hours in the self-help aisle at Barnes and Noble, researching an antidote to my crippling fear of myself and my identity. Was I in a quarter-life crisis? I certainly felt like I was. There was only so much psychological theory that my mind could absorb before learning became insidiously frustrating. I gained what amounted to a decent academic knowledge of my issues, but it didn't have the power to deliver me from the bondage of pain, anxiety, and worthlessness I felt. Obtaining information about my maladies and exploring the why behind my experiences only drove me to further insanity. I could find temporary answers and seek out a certain understanding, but self-help books are a dime a dozen, and a huge profit-making industry bolsters the psychology market. I read advice and analysis that made complete and total sense but still left me hardened and hurt. I felt the more knowledge I gained about my situation only gave me more stones to throw at people and confirm my victimization. It allowed me to justifiably build a wall around my heart to those who had hurt me deeply. The books pertaining to life crises, ten steps to *this*, eight steps to *that*, helped me see that I needed healing, but they never provided it.

Life was beckoning me to come clean with myself, to face the hard facts of where I was, what I was doing, and where I was headed. I was headed straight on a path to a literal hell on earth. I would have to look trauma in the face, stare at it long and hard and let the root of bitterness, rejection, anger and fear go. The realization that my inner workings needed a good Drano treatment for all the sludge and slough accumulated through years of living apart from the sustaining grace of God brought me to a level of desperation that I needed to begin healing.

It was then I knew I would have to face the scary reality. I knew I needed what was planted in me as a child: Jesus. It was a knowing in my inner being, like when you know someone is staring at you from across the room. I needed a Savior that spoke to my inner need for safety, love, and comfort. The funny thing is I didn't know that my Savior was loving, comforting and safe. I had relied on the religious doctrine I learned as a child, and ironically, it kept me away from Jesus for years. This doctrine led me to believe I was doomed if I sinned at all, and I believed I would have to work myself back into grace to be loved. In my mind, I tried to reckon Jesus wasn't the way because it seemed impossibly challenging to work myself to fit a mold that I didn't even begin to know how to conform into. After all, I had tried and failed repeatedly to make myself better without any luck; therefore, this God would have to make some exceptions, because in my heart, I knew I needed Him but didn't know how to find Him. How could He accept someone like me who constantly failed? However, despite my questions, I couldn't shake the "knowing in my knower" that I needed Him.

I remember sitting in the back room at work studying something about Daoism, Hinduism, and Buddhism. Mind you, I worked for a Christian woman whose son is a pastor and whose daughter is a well-known Christian vocal artist. One of the owners asked what I was reading about, and I replied something to the effect of how chanting would make me closer to God. She smiled, somewhat laughed and replied, "You don't need chanting: you need Jesus."

I knew I needed Jesus, but the Jesus I had grown up with wasn't a Jesus I wanted a relationship with. He was religious and uptight. He demanded His way, and I felt that with Him in my life, I wouldn't have any fun. I feared His chastisement and anger since I had lived apart from Him for so long, and I'd left church because I could never live up to His high standards of perfection. He was far off anyhow, and from that distance, I believed He must have a smirk on His face, daring me to sin against Him. He asked too much, so why bother since I'm doomed to hell, anyway. "Yeah, right," I thought. "Take your Jesus with you."

However, I couldn't deny this woman always had a glow about her. Her smile radiated with the most beautiful brilliance. As she sat up front booking appointments, she swayed back and forth as if a lullaby soothed her soul. Maybe she did have a point, but how would I get to Him? How was I supposed to look for Him? Certainly not at church. Church only left me feeling more condemned in the first place and set an unattainable bar I could never reach.

What I didn't realize at that point is that God had positioned me in a setting for a breakthrough to get to know Him. What I had known about Him was filtered through the eyes of religion. I know now He sees us through the eyes of grace, mercy, and love. God wanted to peel off the lens of religion, show me His grace and mercy through relationship, and show me who I was, as made in His image, woven as an intricate masterpiece in the hands of the potter of grace. He would take me back to my beginning and the beginning of His Word in Genesis to reveal how I had gotten where I was by way of sin. He wanted to renew and remake me as He did with Adam and Eve. He wanted to show me through the way of wisdom and revelation in His Word how I could be restored through faith and receive an abundant life in Him.

Eventually, through daily reading and meditating on God's Word, I practiced renewing my mind. Through weekly sessions with a Christian therapist, solid in the faith, I was able to take individual lies about myself, others and God and replace them with the life-saving truth of the Gospel that has saved my soul.

If you've come to your end or are seeking an end to the way you are living, there is good news. There is life beyond your discontentment and wandering soul. There is an invitation into a greater, meaningful, full life in a place where passion meets purpose and love, joy, peace, prosperity and meaning flourish. It's a place to bury all guilt and shame in the grave, where you can lay the past behind once and for all and live a completely new life. It's where you can come out from behind a false sense of self and actualize who you are and why you are here. See, the hole you dig apart from grace is a graveside you have been creating where you can dispose of a lifestyle you never have to live again. This six-feet-under you've found yourself captured in is really the beginning point for a new life. In Christ, we are buried with Him and then made alive in Him. This grave will be the site you dance upon one day. He will elevate your life out of this grave, and you'll dance upon it. A marker behind it will say, "This life is no longer! I've been given a new life, a new name and a new experience." Just as Jesus was resurrected from the grave, you will walk right out of your sinful ways and be given a new lease on life. How do I know? I've experienced it for myself. I cannot remain changed and *not* allow this life-giving message to move forward to save many more for the kingdom of God and His Christ in these last days.

God wants to release you from the things in your life that have caged you behind prison walls. These erected, fortified fortresses have been manufactured to keep you "safe" but are the very things that keep you from an abundant life: fear, anxiety, anger, rage, and addiction. The overflow of these "safeguards" are shame, guilt and condemnation. The good news is that Jesus isn't scared of your deep, dark secrets. He's been to hell and back and retrieved the keys of the kingdom to give you entry into the kingdom of heaven here on earth.

I will share with you how the Father met with me, as He did with Adam and Eve in the garden, and how He longs to meet you to begin to mend and rebuild your life from the ground up. His message of restoration and revival has provoked such a strong revelation for me in the last few years, and I want to use everything within me to release the invitation in such a way that an echo of the Father's love ignites a flame in your spirit. He wants to shake all that's shakeable inside you, so all that is left is a place from which to build a firm foundation, which is only found in Christ Jesus. He wants to expose the lies you've believed so He can dismantle the strongholds and replace them with transformational truth about who you were created to be in Jesus.

I am so excited to go alongside you on this journey and take back territory that has either been given to or stolen by the enemy. I want to see everything false replaced with what God originally designed when He created you in your mother's womb. The enemy is *not* victorious over the grave nor the final authority in the trajectory of your life. He only has power over what you allow. But Christ has already bought and redeemed your life, making it possible to live a completely different life. It is from the victory Jesus won that we will rise up as mighty warriors and overcome. Under the name above all names, we take our right position to rule and reign over the darkness disposed of once and for all on Calvary. If this is not exciting, I don't know what is. Freedom is peace; it is heaven on earth.

The religious spirit is being broken off the church by the Holy Spirit of God that moves in holy fire and love, burning the truth of His power into the inner beings of His beloved bride. The truth of Christ and the power to save is being released in a fresh outpouring of deliverance. I believe the new era ushered in simultaneously with the COVID crisis is birthing a new church. It's rebuilding its strength and power as a moving entity, a body built by the Lord with the power of the

Holy Spirit to break off chains and bondages. We are going to see captives set free by the spoken words of Christ Himself. Do you know that is what the gospel means? It is the Word of God unto us. It's news that seems too good to be true, but it is true! Once you hear the Word, I pray you will receive it and let the power it has break chains off your life and deliver you from anything and everything that holds you back from living a fulfilling and whole life. The Word itself is power, the power unto life free from sin and its hold on you.

Jesus read His mission statement, which is found in the book of Isaiah, aloud in the temple:

> The Spirit of the Sovereign LORD is on me,
> because the Lord has anointed me
> to proclaim good news to the poor.
> He has sent me to bind up the brokenhearted,
> to proclaim freedom for the captives
> and release from darkness for the prisoners,
> to proclaim the year of the Lord's favor
> and the day of vengeance of our God,
> to comfort all who mourn,
> and provide for those who grieve in Zion—
> to bestow on them a crown of beauty
> instead of ashes,
> the oil of joy
> instead of mourning,
> and a garment of praise
> instead of a spirit of despair.
> (Isaiah 61:1–4, NIV)

Now is the time of your favor, your redemption. It is your time for love and deliverance by the God that heals, that binds up your wounds and releases deep healing in the places of your soul (your mind, will and emotions) that were damaged by sin—your sin and the sin done to you by others. He's done this for me, and I know He will do the same for you. You will have to give from your end, adjust your schedule, and surrender your thoughts, opinions and beliefs, but it's all worth the freedom He gives. The God that originally formed you in secret in your mother's womb is calling you to the secret place of His presence to make you new. Go away with Him, find a place to sit alone and allow His grace and mercy to heal your wounds. Find a fellowship of believers that love Jesus, and let them lock arms and pray with you. Jesus ever lives to make intercession for you to the Father (Hebrews 7:5). He is doing it even now: He is championing your breakthrough!

Dear beloved, I hope downloads of revelation from the love of God begin to bombard your spirit through His supreme mercy and grace as you read through these pages. I'll take you on my journey where I surrendered and began coming back to Jesus. Jesus wants the same for you. He accepts us in our fallen nature and sets us on higher ground, the rock of His stability, secure and firm. He gives you a new name, a righteous name because anyone who comes to Him by faith is a rightful heir to His throne. Through grace you have been saved by faith, not because of anything you have done but because He loved you so much He died for you and placed His love on you. He paid the full price and gave you unmerited favor to receive eternal life. How is that for a beautiful exchange? You only need to believe and receive.

Let's pray. Father, I thank you for your Word. Thank you for the power available through your Word to teach, instruct, and liberate us. Your presence and eternal purpose of love let us know who you are so we can know who we are in you. Father, we give you time and space in our hearts to do what only you can do. Holy Spirit, come alive in us as we pore over these pages. Illuminate what you want to speak over our lives. In Jesus' mighty and holy name. Amen!

Chapter 2—

THE CHASE

What do you think? If a man owns a hundred sheep, and one of them wanders away, will he not leave the ninety-nine on the hills and go to look for the one that wandered off?
(Matthew 18:12, NIV)

One Sunday morning, I was out running. It was my typical routine to unwind from a hard week. The fall season had just begun, and the refreshing temperature made it optimal for a long-distance run. I chose a route that would lead me from my small apartment along industrial roads to downtown. There and back was a six-mile loop. On my circuit home, I stopped at a red light at a large intersection. I had taken my iPod off my armband to adjust what I was listening to when I felt a car come so close it brushed against my arm. A mom driving a minivan had run up onto the curb. Mere millimeters kept the van from running me over. The driver had managed to keep me alive but scared the living daylights out of me. I'm not sure she was aware of what happened. As she maneuvered through the intersection, I saw her peering into her rearview mirror and screaming at her children in the backseat.

A lady watching from her front porch across the street saw the incident. She screamed out in a panic, asking if I was ok. "Yes, I'm fine," I replied. She asked if I needed a ride home, but I did not take the offer. I was certainly shaken up, but I knew finishing the run would bring a calmness to my beating heart.

A song came on my iPod. Remember me saying my boss' daughter was a Christian music singer? It was one of her songs. As I trekked toward home, I knew God was calling out to me through that song. I'd just experienced His divine protection, and I knew it wasn't a coincidence.

Normally after a run, I go home, stretch, make an egg white sandwich and take a nap. However, that day was different. First, I felt an internal nudge… "Go to church." Then, a warring struggle: "NO." I was more worried about what to wear and how people would receive me than about what the pastor's message might be. After all, aren't you supposed to dress your best? Dress the part of a put-together citizen of society? I certainly could do that, but I would feel like a fraud. However, I pressed past the chatter in my mind and went anyway.

As soon as I entered the church, I was greeted by warm, welcoming folks. Their cheerful smiles and comforting handshakes made the awkwardness I felt in attending less distressing. The service began with praise and worship music. People filed down to the altar to sing and dance. Why the lifting of hands and singing loudly? I wondered. The dancing and shouting without hesitation? In the Baptist church I grew up in, congregants stood up and sat down; there was no lifting of hands, no shouting, and no dancing. If you did, you would be seen as a fool and escorted out by a man in a suit. These people seemed to be filled with something I surely wasn't. That day, the sermon made a little bit of sense to me, but there was so much about the Bible I didn't comprehend. I felt lost in storylines and the unfamiliar names highlighted by the pastor's text.

After a few months of routinely visiting the church, I met my husband, Bill, through the internet dating site, Match.com. I was embarrassed to tell him I believed in Christ, thinking he would shun me. My faith had become so precious to me, and I didn't want to be judged by it.

After a Saturday evening date, Bill asked what I was doing the following day.

I reluctantly replied, "Church."

"Do you mind if I go with you?"

That hurdle was passed, and we began attending church together weekly. While the pastor gave the sermon, I would nestle under Bill's shoulder and feel the warmth and comfort of love's requited bliss.

It was a Thursday evening when my then-fiancé suggested we try a new church—a megachurch established a few years prior. They had their own program on mainstream TV. My first instinct was to say yes, but then—no. No, I thought, that church is big and intimidating. The one we attended was small and intimate. In my mind, I forecasted a large crowd of cheerful, put-together people. Large crowds had always made me feel uneasy. The more people around, the more paranoia and uneasiness aggravated my inner world. My interior panic alarm would alert me, dizziness would encircle me, and tingling sensations would rise in my chest, arms and legs. What if they could see through me, how messed up I really was? I didn't feel like putting up a front to try something new when our church was already sufficient. No, No. No. I would not go.

God knew what He was doing when He put me with my firecracker fiancé; Bill is anything but shy. He's a fierce provocateur who stands up to a challenge whenever it's presented. He knew how scary a new church would be for me. Eventually, I agreed to try it, and he encouraged me every step of the way.

I remember getting there and meeting two of his friends. My state of panic was severe; I knew it was obvious. My mouth felt like it was quivering. My hands and underarms oozed sweat like an open spigot. I knew my legs would buckle at any moment. I clung to Bill's arm for dear life. I begged him not to leave my side nor take his hand from mine because of the fear that I might pass out. Not being drunk (as I typically would have been when I knew I had to be in an anxiety-producing atmosphere—but I didn't want to be drunk at church!) left me feeling even more vulnerable. Luckily, I found myself in a dark, almost concert-like atmosphere once we entered the sanctuary. I felt a little more comfortable since I could literally hide myself in the venue.

The band got on stage, and the performance began. It was unlike anything I had ever experienced before. It was a full, live concert, but one for Jesus. Everyone stood, and most everyone sang. I felt uninhibited, unashamed and free. I didn't have to worry about my posture, how off-key I was singing or crying, for that matter, because no one could see me. I felt a presence like I'd never felt in church because I was able to let my guard down, sing and worship as I had seen others do in the church we had been going to. But there, in the light of the sanctuary, I'd felt too ashamed to let my guard down.

The preacher didn't preach like anyone I'd ever heard. Instead, he spoke of challenges, and people responded with clapping, amens and hallelujahs. The atmosphere of worship felt alive! For once in my life, I felt the tangible, palpable feeling that I know now is freedom's presence—a freedom that I've learned is only in Christ.

After the service, I couldn't wait to return again. I wanted to know more. In my gut, I knew this church would be the gateway for the healing I desperately needed. The first glimmer of breakthrough was a glimpse of a burgeoning new life just around the corner.

Chapter 3—

BREAKDOWN TO BREAKTHROUGH

Your eyes saw my unformed body;
all the days ordained for me were written in
your book
before one of them came to be.
(Psalm 139:16, NIV)

I t was mid-July; my fiancé and I had decided to take the plunge and move in together after only five short months of dating. But issues began surfacing in our relationship, and our disagreements were at an all-time high. I saw any conflict as a threat to my safety and survival. I interpreted it a possible ending to a relationship instead viewing it as an opportunity to gain insight into the heart of another or myself. I saw it as a threat of rejection and abandonment. As a small child, I had learned to keep the peace at any cost. If I didn't, I feared I would lose the love of my loved ones.

Later, I escaped the awful pain of perceived, potential abandonment through drinking. I was not emotionally adept at handling conflict, so I buried myself in alcohol and cigarettes. Alcohol numbed the pain before any distress could hit me. When alcohol wasn't enough to soothe my hurt, I became physically abusive. If we were going to knock each other out with words, I might as well use my fists, too. Overwhelmed by perceived threats, I've thrown shoes, slammed doors hard enough to break the glass, and kicked in trash cans. When I was triggered, it was like my emotions were hijacked. Any conflict instigated my fight, flight, or freeze response. There was nothing in me to act as a gauge to slow, stop, or work around it. I only knew how to execute the conflict by engaging in destructive behavior.

On this particular night, I didn't have the choice to flee, smoke, or drink. I was stuck, caged, and highly emotional, with no outlet to calm my rage. Desperate to quell the storm, I went upstairs to the bathroom to kick and rage in private. A thought came to me: *What if I cut away the pain?* I took a pair of scissors from my fiancé's drawer and thrashed the blades across my wrist until I saw blood. As soon as the blade cut through my wrist, pain writhed out of my arm as blood dripped on the floor.

I was suddenly overcome with shame and grief that shook me to the core.

A heavy flow of tears poured out. *Why would I do that? Why?* I went from trying to escape one kind of pain to feeling the lowest of all lows. My thoughts were so messed up. I didn't know right from left. I didn't know up from down. I just knew I wanted this cycle of agony to stop. I needed a way out of the labyrinth of pain. It seemed too complicated to find a way to set my life in the right direction, to abate the gnawing, internal despair and toxic shame. I shrunk to a fetal position on the cold bathroom floor, confused, tired, and defeated.

"Jesus!" I screamed.

What happened next was something I had read about in books but never experienced myself. As I sat there clutching my wrist, keeping the blood from running out, I cried out, "Jesus, Jesus, I need you! I don't know if you exist, but I need you. Please help me, please, I need you," I bawled.

In that instant, I felt a presence walk into that bathroom. A calming peace blanketed over me like newly fallen snow. I heard a soft, tender voice in my heart: "It's ok. I'm here now."

I had no clue what this meant or even what I was experiencing, but I knew it was something. I knew that Jesus knew. Somehow, I trusted that this inward voice I felt was Jesus and that He had responded to my call. In the rawness of the moment, I felt Him encouraging me to get up and get help. Get up and stand up, no matter how wobbly it felt. To do something about this hole, this hell in my head, the lifestyle crumbling around me. It hit me as if a light bulb, for the first time, knew how to shine.

This Jesus was real! I didn't want to leave the bathroom, for it was the first time I'd felt the tangible presence of peace in a long time. Thoughts ran through my head. *How would I get there? How would I feel Him again? How would I know Him?* He seemed so close, but still so far away—a mystical reality, but reality, nonetheless. How could this strange experience be replicated? I knew I was messed up. Very messed up. I desperately wanted more of that peace that fell over me when I called His name.

His presence was a like a tranquil infusion of peace that transposed fear from every fiber within my being. A warmth was radiant within my heart as if the lover of my life had summoned me to come away with Him. I was consumed.

Two words stuck on repeat in my head as I picked myself up off the ground: *mercy* and *grace*. Mercy, meaning His forgiveness and pardon of my sin, and grace, His unmerited favor to redeem my life through the unearned fellowship of communion through which I would receive His power to overcome my maladies. I had no deep understanding or revelation of what the two words meant at the time, but a clearer understanding would come the closer the fellowship I developed with Him over time.

***

One evening, while surfing through a barrage of Facebook streams, I came across Sarah Reeves' remake of Hillsong's popular song, "Oceans." It spoke to me like Christ's living Word. I encourage you to listen to the song if you're unfamiliar with it. In the lyrics, the ocean and waves are analogies for the faith that is possible through Christ. When God picked me up off the bathroom floor that fateful night, He gave me hope that life was possible. The sense I received was to keep moving forward—God was calling me out on the water, as in "Oceans," and as Jesus had called Peter. He beckoned me to press forward with hope toward life in the direction He was taking me. With faith, I accepted His offer. With weariness in my spirit, he gave me just what I needed to take one step forward and keep living, moment by moment, day by day. It was the start of something beautiful. Deep down, I knew I would never be the same.

I knew there was power in calling out His name, Jesus. He answered my request to come, and He continues to teach me more about Him and heal and mend the brokenness that got me to the extreme depths of desperation. Only He could start make the repairs.

His presence is what I know now as the working of the Holy Spirit. His voice began guiding my life in a new direction. I was marked that day as a blood-bought citizen of grace by the precious blood of Jesus. I had a fire in my soul, a thirst in my spirit, a longing and an unspeakable desire to know more about the life Jesus offers.

The Father meets us where we are. He is not ashamed to meet us even in the pits of utter hell and desperation.

The sacrifice you desire is a broken spirit.
You will not reject a broken and repentant heart, O God. (Psalm 51:17, NLT)

Chapter 4—

LAY IT ON THE ALTAR

I have chosen the way of truth;
I have set your ordinances before me.
I cling to your testimonies, O LORD;
let me not be put to shame.
(Psalm 119:30–31, BSB)

I faced a difficult but necessary challenge of whether to halt my engagement and move home with my mom. To fully receive what God had prepared for me, I needed to step away from the path I was on. This gut decision—move home or marry now—kept playing in the back of my mind, and nothing I did would get it to stop. The Holy

Spirit asked me to lay my relationship on the altar and allow God to lead me. As hard and as scary as it was to possibly lose the man I loved and adored, I moved back to my childhood home.

As I sorted through my childhood closet to organize my belongings, I came across many Christian books. My mom stored them anywhere and everywhere, in nooks and crannies around the house. As a child, I recognized she was a believer, but I never really gave it much thought. "That's for older people," I thought at the time, thus disregarding the issue.

I began picking the books up and reading the back covers to see what they entailed. Suddenly the voice came back, the same one from the bathroom. A feeling came to me like I had picked up on something. I began reading pages in the books, and it was as if words of wisdom were highlighted for me, instructing me on what to do next. The words had a whole new meaning and a whole new life to them. The books became life to my body and health to my bones (Proverbs 3:8).

> My son, give attention to my words;
> Incline your ear to my sayings.
> Do not let them depart from your sight;
> Keep them in the midst of your heart.
> For they are life to those who find them
> And health to all their flesh.
> Keep your heart with all diligence,
> For out of it spring the issues of life.
> (Proverbs 4:20–23, NKJV)

My inspiration for this book came as the Lord took me back to the beginning of the Word, to the garden where Adam and Eve sinned. Adam and Eve were created naked and without shame (Genesis 2:25). Suddenly, their eyes were opened, and they knew the shame of nakedness apart from the Lord's glory covering. Father God approached His beloved Adam, the firstborn son of humanity, with this question: "Who told you you were naked?" (Genesis 3:11, TLB). It began a conversation about why Adam hid. How did Adam recognize his human condition of nakedness and seek to escape Father's presence? Until that time, they walked in complete unity, in nakedness and complete vulnerability with one another. The garden, which God created for Adam and his mate Eve to live in, was perfect! It was a utopia: they were provided for, cared for, and dwelled in perfect communion with the Father. He carefully designed the garden so that Adam and Eve would have everything at their disposal.

As sin exposed their nakedness, the knowledge of disobedience struck Adam and Eve to their cores; it touched the essence of their identity. Oh, how I knew this truth! The nakedness of shame had been a plaguing mainstay for me. I felt raw and exposed—like people could read my mail and see how awful I was as I repeatedly sinned. I had no power to resist or stop the urge: rebellion had a vise-like grip on me. Shame, guilt and condemnation overflowed in my life, and I felt like an utter failure. Like an abandoned house, my property was filled with critters, weeds and the like that assumed occupancy. My mind was filled with vile thoughts toward myself and others. My life reflected the overflow of this negative self-chatter. A literal death had taken over my soul, and I found it hard to believe that this good God could ever approve of a vile person like me. This lie gave the enemy access, and he obtained a foothold, which became a stronghold. Strongholds are places in our minds fortified by negative beliefs. These lies became fortresses of misperceptions that attempted to lock my soul in darkness, a place of misunderstanding, a bottomless abyss of obstinance, self-rejection and abandonment.

As sin began in my life so I could see how my sinful nature was directly affecting me through my original DNA. I had inevitably run out of me and fallen into the rock of ages, Jesus. It wasn't something weird or to be ashamed of—no, it happens to the best of us. I was born into a fallen world where sin abounds.

Understanding what happened in the garden gave me perspective.

I wasn't weird or odd. I was just ignorant of the enemy's devices and schemes. I was unaware of the snares and traps set before me to lure me into the lair of his will, deception and ultimate death. The Word says that the enemy seeks who he may devour, that he is an accuser of the brethren. He comes to steal, kill and destroy, and cut lives short from experiencing the truth of who God is. The enemy had been caught, and his devices uncovered.

God took me through the process of enlightening my eyes to the truth that would bring transformational healing. The glory of God's grace began working in me, shifting the self-hatred I had acquiesced to for so long to see I was born with a plan and purpose. I wasn't an accident; I wasn't a misfit. I was just way off course from the will of God.

I just needed a chance. I needed Jesus—the Way.

***

While Bill and I lived apart, we frequently dated one another. He wasn't happy that I'd uprooted and moved back to my mother's house, but he understood I wasn't in a good space mentally and needed focused time to heal. We still attended church as a couple and even joined an at-home group together. We also individually attended eGroups to grow amongst peers who had similar passions to follow the way of Jesus. I was introduced to a women's group leader described as "zealous for the Lord" and as "eccentric" for things of Jesus. I thought, *What does that even mean?* It was intriguing, though. Maybe she was the real deal, not puffed up on religion or dead works. As a deep thinker practically from birth, I needed someone eccentric and zealous to answer the theological questions swirling around in my mind. Her sincerity and what she presented about Jesus nestled deep within my spirit and provoked an even deeper desire to study the Word on my own. She introduced me to the activation and impartation of the Word through prayer. In meetings, we read and discussed the Word and ended with a prayer circle. I would leave on fire for the things of God, thirsting to return and learn more.

Immersing myself in Christian culture and sacrificing time to retrain my brain to the truth was delivering me from self-harming thoughts. However, the stubborn strongholds of anger and addiction to alcohol and cigarettes weren't budging. I knew I would have to delve into therapy, but hopefully, from a different approach than I had previously experienced. God provided.

A lady who attended the weekly Wednesday night meetings suggested an inner healing, Christian therapist she had been consulting. I was reluctant to call because my last therapist left me wary about opening up to someone again. Her comments about my disorders left me feeling bereft and hopeless that I'd ever change. She even said that I shouldn't have kids to create this problem again. Yet, however hesitant I was, my focused priority was to recover. What was the worst that could happen? A new therapist could tell me I was crazy out of my mind, too?

I booked an appointment. I sat in the hot seat of confession and explained my outbursts of anger, the bubbling lava of fire that was provoked when anger arose, and my battle with alcohol and cigarettes that wouldn't abate. No matter how much I loved and adored Jesus, the cravings wouldn't cease.

I knew she was different than any other therapist when she read my mail. Driven by the Holy Spirit, she quickly discerned my issues and began a discourse laying the necessary groundwork to allow me to experience true freedom in Christ. She identified co-dependency as the root of my issues, which made complete sense after she explained the cycles of failure of that mindset. Her mission and commission with the Holy Spirit were to unravel the lies that kept me in anger's strong vise. Why was I driven to such strong emotion every time I was frustrated, offended, or perceived rejection and abandonment?

Week after week, we weeded through my thoughts, dismantling false perceptions of God, others and myself. Forgiveness was the start of almost every session. When we experience trauma, whether self-induced or from the treachery of others, a lens begins to form, shaping how we perceive the world. This lens creates a paradigm of how we believe God operates and how we communicate with others and relate to ourselves. Once the trauma is dealt with, the lens automatically lifts and a new reality forms.

My journals revealed that I saw God through the lenses of rejection and abandonment from my father, a demand for perfectionism from my mother, and at a distance from how others treated me. Healing prayers and the activation of hearing God's voice would transform how I thought God saw me. The joyful truth is that His countenance is one of love towards me, and it is for you, too. Because of love, He redeems and restores us despite our sins, iniquities and transgressions.

These precepts laid a new foundation in my mind. As I re-routed my thoughts through a restored framework, my desires began changing, my anger was not being stirred as often, and a regenerated inner voice of positive self-talk was emerging.

I will never forget a session when I was delivered from the spirit of anger. Just before my appointment that day, I had a fallout with my fiancé. I was furious—a perfect setup to be counseled through. The roaring storm within brewed beneath the surface. However, I had developed enough self-control to place time between my triggers and acting out. Lots of time, actually, and I was grateful for that. I explained what had taken place. I told my therapist I wanted to quit reacting that way anymore; I wanted the skill to respond appropriately. As we prayed together, she got the unction to anoint my head with oil and pray the spirit of anger off me. As she prayed, I felt a fierce scream begin to boil in my stomach.

I asked if it was ok if I screamed at the top of my lungs (the therapist's office was in a three-story business complex).

"If that's what you feel, let it out," she exclaimed.

The screech belted from the uttermost depths of my stomach and thundered through her modest office. Following the scream came an unexpected flow, a torrent of tears. The counselor knelt over my fragile frame and held me like a baby until the convulsions of dry heaving left. All the trauma, all the anger from feeling used, abused, beaten, tread upon, misunderstood, and devalued all came up in one big heave. I felt the lightest inside I had ever felt. The presence of peace I'd felt on the cold, white tile from the bathroom appeared again.

That marked the day the rage was gone. It's been almost eight years, and that feeling hasn't returned. Glory to God.

A full year-and-a-half of weekly Wednesday recovery meetings had catapulted me from darkness into accessing the light of truth from the kingdom of God.

Chapter 5—

BACK TO THE BEGINNING

There is not one person who can hide their thoughts from God, for nothing that we do remains a secret, and nothing created is concealed, but everything is exposed and defenseless before his eyes, to whom we must render an account. (Hebrews 4:13, TPT)

I grew up in a broken family. My mother became my primary caretaker when my father left us to throw all his efforts into a new career. I was four. Losing my father's presence and seeing the hardships my mother went through to raise me as a single parent burdened my heart. Fortunately, my mother had a great career and a steady income, but having a good job is just the beginning of providing care for a child. Children have intense emotional needs because they haven't developed coping skills to work through feelings. They require adults to help them manage, sort through and process big emotions. Seeing my mom struggle and feeling abandoned by my father, I fell into a deep pit of self-loathing.

I thought, *If only I wasn't here. Maybe I caused the divorce. Maybe I'm such a bad child, they couldn't get along.* My mom seemed burdened and downcast. She tried explaining that none of it was my fault, but from my childlike perspective, I begged to differ. My father moved on so easily—or so I thought. He eventually remarried and took care of his new wife's three children. In addition to those new stepsiblings, I had an older half-sister from my dad's previous marriage before my mom. To say I felt out of place and an oddball in my new family structure is an understatement. I didn't know where I fit into my dad's heart: he had four other children—three stepchildren and one half-sister to take in hand.

When I visited him on appointed weekends and holidays, I felt I didn't fit in with the patterns of his new home. I wanted to, of course, but my shyness and quiet demeanor made forming quality relationships with my half and stepsiblings challenging. When I was away from my mom, I felt especially vulnerable to rejection. I struggled with liking who I was because I felt uncomfortable in my new surroundings.

My mom remarried when I was ten. Her new husband had two children, both younger than I was. So I went from being an only child, living with my mom, occasionally seeing my half and stepsiblings from my dad's side, to constantly seeing stepsiblings at my mom's as well. It was just how things were; I had no voice, so I went along with everything as it was dealt.

Being a child of divorced parents is just flat-out hard. Maybe that's you, and you've had these same thoughts, too. Maybe you've believed them to the point of thinking you're flawed, bad, shamed, or not enough. Then, when the love you expect from a parent isn't fulfilled, the lie begins: *If I was just _____ (fill in the blank), maybe I would be worthy of love.* Perhaps your parents are still together, but there was always a sibling comparison going on, so you can relate.

I felt ostracized from the life I knew, and I was spiraling downward from the abrupt changes at home and school. As if middle school years weren't tough enough, I had to switch school systems.

The road my parents had built their home on transferred school districts my fifth-grade year. The year my mom remarried, I was bussed a long distance to help make up the white percentage in a predominantly African American school. On the first day of school, I complimented a girl on her weave. (I'd asked a cousin of mine who was bussed there, too, what was different about their hair.) She replied, "Shut up, white girl." I felt so rejected, so out of place. After attending a majority-white country school, I was in culture shock. The students in my new school had a way of communicating that I wasn't used to, and they didn't seem welcoming.

Upon returning from school that evening, I begged my mom to not make me go back. I hated how rude and loud the kids were. At the time, I was an extreme rule abider, a teacher's pet. I did anything for them to approve of me so I could feel accepted. I was an average B-student with struggles in math and social sciences. Getting C or D in these classes was a strong probability. I thought to myself, *If I could just be more well-rounded and good at everything, I would feel better. If I could just get all A's, my parents would be proud of me.*

I eventually made friends at the new school, but the ones I spent more time hanging out with weren't the best influences. Their parents drank and smoked in their homes, which I had never been accustomed to.

During these years, I struggled with my weight. I wasn't really aware of using food as an escape, but I grew up with jelly biscuits and pot roast as mainstays in my diet. Growing up southern with a caretaker whose delight was making anything that involved butter and sugar quickly added pounds to my frame that easily gains weight.

Both my parents were quite thin and fit. They'd comment on how much I ate and how I should exercise to keep from gaining weight. I felt rejected. They ate the same things and remained thin while I ate them and blew up like a balloon. *Maybe I'm too fat. Maybe they're embarrassed to be my parents because I'm not as cute as they'd like me to be. If only I could be thinner, they would be more proud of me.* My insecurities were compounded by my thin, in shape half and stepsiblings, who received compliments on how pretty they were all the time. I believed if I was thinner and fit, I'd be accepted.

I always had a sense I was different than everyone else. Others my age were hanging out and doing age-appropriate activities, but I was in the corner, just wanting an in-depth conversation. I would go to a sleepover at a friend's house and end up engaging in conversation with the parents just as much as the girl my age. I loved the maturity of adulthood and was innately inquisitive about what it would be like. However, my interest made me feel ostracized when it came time to be with a group of peers. I was always curious: how were they so carefree—playing outside, playing with friends? When you feel different, it can create a feeling of lack and worthlessness. I questioned my values and internal makeup. *Why can't I just fit in? Why do I feel so awkward hanging around kids my age?*

Any child who has had unfortunate things happen without someone to talk them through it can believe that their life was a mistake.

Desperate to Fit In

At fourteen, I attended a party where drinking was involved. I had never had a sip of alcohol and didn't know what it would do to me. Feeling pressured to try a beverage, I took one. Immediately, I felt different. My typical shy awkwardness turned into freedom and boldness. The protective layer I had hidden behind suddenly gave way to a more confident and relaxed me.

An older guy had his eyes on me from across the room. He asked my name. For the first time, I felt desirable. (Until then, I felt like a guy never looked at me, much less asked me to be his girlfriend.) Then, he asked the girl I was with if I was available.

She said, "Yes, you should talk to her."

I don't remember much about our conversation, but I remember what happened after another drink. He asked me to go back to his dorm room. There, kissing led to taking my clothes off, to being held down on his bed. I remember feeling awful and dirty. I remember wanting to punch him, even though deep inside, I had felt wanted. It was too much for my fourteen-year-old brain to process. I had no choice but to take the thrusts of his pelvic region into mine.

We both got dressed, and he took me back to my friend's house. I remember running inside and asking for a pad. I was spotting, bleeding and explaining to her what had happened through tears.

"It's ok; we've all done it," she said, trying to reassure me.

The next day I remember feeling ashamed, but I didn't tell anyone else because I feared punishment.

That escapade opened a door for sexuality to pervert what would attract males to me for the next decade. In the attempt to feel worthwhile, I threw my worth away into the arms of guy after guy, hoping to receive the love and acceptance I longed for. As the pain of shame ate away at me, I gave myself to guy after guy. I lost any sense of value. I had become someone guys just wanted to sleep with. I had resigned myself to the belief that for any guy to like me, I had to be sexual. That invited a whole lot of other substitutes to take away the emptiness and void within.

Outwardly, I pulled myself together. My grades might have suffered a little, but I remained a B student. I engaged in extracurricular activities, like tennis and cheerleading. My friend group was just about everyone. I secretly wanted to be popular just so I would feel accepted.

Eventually, drinking became my numbing device to cover up all the shame and pain. I added smoking as well. Cigarettes became an outlet to relieve my extreme anxiety.

***

Directly and indirectly via media, I received the consistent message that I was *less than*, so I felt I needed to strive to be *more*. Of course, I can't speak for other people's interpretation and how it plays out for them, but a strategy of striving and perfectionism drove a seed deep into my soul. The seed was planted there from a young age. I felt that I had to present myself with outward perfection to be of any value or interest to others. By 18, I found myself in a restrictive food obsession. What began as a clever way of counting calories for knowledge became an obsessive number game with the scale.

Each night as I undressed to shower, I examined my enlarged thighs, saggy butt dimpled with cellulite and arms in the mirror. Pinching my fat, I wondered, *Why can't I be thin like the girls in the magazines?* In my mind, I was still a chubby, out-of-shape preteen. Ironically, I had become excessively skinny like the waif like runway models I admired. My previous full-body image distorted reality: my malnourished body was thin and gaunt.

Memories of being teased and ridiculed by peers had a lasting impression on my body image and self-esteem. My father's comments on what I ate and my weight issues added to my negative body image.

"It's the Ingle syndrome, Elizabeth. You have to be careful what you eat." (Ingle was my original last name.) The constant reminders became an obsession: I would do whatever possible to keep my weight down.

I desperately wanted to fit in and be called beautiful. I wanted to mirror the image of women I idolized in the *Victoria's Secret* catalog and the fashion models that graced the runways. I wanted the fame and the attention those women received. But mainly, I wanted someone to look at me and be astounded, think I was gorgeous, and tell me so. I knew I wouldn't believe it was true, but I wanted someone to point it out, so I could somehow piece together the actuality of it in my mind.

For years, I battled my weight. I tried every magic diet, diet pills, exercise—you name it, I had done it. I used my body as an experimental device to figure out the best weight loss plan. But nothing gave a lasting fix. My weight constantly fluctuated 10–15 pounds.

In my senior year of high school, I told myself I would tackle my weight once and for all. I would research foods, inform myself of what I was eating and how many calories I consumed. I discovered the calories in, calories out method for weight loss. It seemed to be a more logical approach to weight control than previous means I had tried. Before, I had watched what I was eating by counting fat grams and eliminating sweets. But there was no real methodology in what I was doing to diet. If I was going to lose weight, I would have to educate myself on food and portion control.

For months, I continued my approach, but instead of weight dropping like it had previously, it plateaued. I found myself feeling antsy again. How could I take my knowledge of food and modify it to start losing again?

The progression toward anorexia is slow. You don't just wake up one morning and decide to restrict food. It's a sickness that develops in the mind over time, like a slow-developing cancer. I realized dieting had become an addiction when my caloric intake became an obsession, not just an observation. I developed a formula for consuming 800 calories or less than I burned in a day. It took discipline to keep my calorie intake at that level, but I felt power and confidence from restricting my body's desire for food. My fatigue and weakness were overpowered by a sense of bodily esteem as the pounds quickly melted off.

The realization that I'd entered a full-blown eating disorder peaked when my weight dropped from 135 to 115 at the beginning of my freshman year of college. For the first time in my life, peers paid what I heard as positive attention to how I looked, commenting on how they wished they were as thin as I. My dad took notice and gave me the attention I had always craved. To hear him say, "You look good, babe," made my day.

Around that time, I signed a modeling contract with a Charlotte talent agency. *I fit in with the skinny girls!* To be honest, this acceptance was fuel to the fire, adding ammunition to my sickness. Instead of being content with myself at a relatively healthy weight, I wanted to see how far I could take it. The sickness in my mind beckoned: *How skinny can I be?* I took it as a challenge to see how much I could lose. I had an inkling at that point that it could be a problem, but I wasn't aware how far I would go or how detrimental the pathway I was on would be.

***

Spring of my freshman year of college rolled around. My weight plummeted to around 100. It was apparent to all that on my athletic build, my weight loss had gone too far. Instead of hearing, "Wow, you look great," I heard, "You're looking kind of thin—are you ok?" But even though I had begun descending this downward spiral at an alarming pace, their words still added fuel to my fire for a time. *Thin.* That felt satisfying.

I remained compulsive about counting every calorie and crumb that entered my body, obsessive about exercising if I ate "too much" that day. I planned every meal to the exact detail. If I was going out to dinner, I would starve all day, so I could consume all my calories that night. It was time-consuming and energy-draining to be so obsessed with my weight. Up to this point, I felt in control of my body and powerful from being able to be so consistent with weight loss.

But now, it had begun to control me. I didn't like the obsessive thoughts or the planning. It was too much work, too draining, but I didn't know how to let go. I didn't know how to get help, and I didn't want to admit to those I loved that I had a problem. I was ashamed and embarrassed to admit it to them and to myself. I recognized I had a problem, but verbally admitting it takes courage, which I didn't have.

***

One morning, my mom entered my room unannounced. I was only wearing my underwear and bra and had bent over to grab something.

When I heard her gasp, I turned to see what was wrong.

"Elizabeth, I can see every bone in your body, honey." She came over to me and hugged my frail frame. Tears welled up in her eyes.

She didn't go any further with a conversation about my appearance until I sat down by her and my stepfather one Sunday afternoon following church.

The following morning, I begrudgingly showed up at the doctor's appointment she'd made me. The nurse checked my weight: 98. My blood pressure: dangerously low. My vitals: in trouble.

The doctor came to the room with the unfortunate results. She first addressed my mom: "She has what's medically diagnosed as anorexia nervosa. It's common in girls around her age and can be overcome. It's going to take time and lots of counseling to figure out the root of what is leading her to do this. I can either send her home with you and you can nurse her back to health, which will require seeing a nutritionist and counselor, or I can send her to rehab."

Then, she addressed me: "Elizabeth, this is your warning: if you want to live, you've got to receive help. You make the decision. We are here to support you in whatever you need and help you get better."

I accepted the threatening offer and agreed to months of therapy and a nutritionist to help rebuild my relationship with food. The nutritionist made suggestions that would allow me to incrementally gain weight to avoid a relapse. She taught me about food as fuel for my body and showed me how and what to eat. I didn't realize what I was previously eating had caused my weight gain. I ate what my mom and dad did, but I was built differently and required a different diet. By the end of my freshman year, I had gained back a healthy ten pounds. I still appeared thin but looked less gaunt. Light was at the end of the tunnel, but I wasn't out of the woods yet.

A summer break spent with a friend in Atlanta allowed the eating disorder to resurface—this time, with more vengeance. Away from home with no parents to harp on me about what or when I was eating, I let my disorder spiral out of control.

I woke up one morning around 3:00 a.m. I barely made it to the toilet fast enough to throw up. It started coming out both ends. Food poisoning, most likely. Weak and barely able to walk, I made it over to the scale to weigh myself: 93. (As I write this, I can feel the chills, just as I did that night.)

I called my mom immediately to tell her goodbye. I honestly thought I was going to die. Her loud sobbing on the other end of the phone scared me even more.

"Elizabeth, we allowed you to go down there because you were getting better. What happened?"

"I don't know, Mom, but I feel like I'm going to die. I wanted to talk to you, in case I do." I felt an overwhelming languish and lethargy down to the core of my bones. I slumped down over the toilet seat and cried until I could cry no longer. After promising I would make a commitment to get better, I hung up.

That night was the start of a new beginning. The doctor's news I had anorexia had scared me, but not as much as lying on that cold tile floor, feeling as if I was taking my last breaths.

I only had a few more weeks till returning home. During my last few weeks in Atlanta, I gained weight and was back up to 100 pounds. It was still not enough, but I felt better and stronger.

I made it safely back home to Salisbury and into counseling again. I slowly became more aware that I was getting better each day. I didn't want to die: I wanted to live. Hitting rock bottom switched the tune of anorexia: by Christmas of my sophomore year, I returned to a healthy weight of 120.

Bulimia—Another Crash Course

I wiped crusted puke from my face and stared at my bloated cheeks in the mirror. Black mascara had run down my cheeks. I looked like a female member of the band KISS.

I stood looking at my reflection for a while, disgusted by the person I saw. In the toilet bowl, remnants of food particles floated in the water.

What are you doing, Elizabeth? How had I let another addiction grab such a tight hold on me? I looked awful, and I felt awful.

I cleaned my face with soap and water and crawled into bed. Another day, another chance to put it behind me. *Tomor-*

row I will stop. I promised myself I'd take control of my bing-
ing and purging episodes. I hated it. I hated the way it made
my throat burn. My mouth tasted awful, and the blood veins
had burst around my eyes. *Please, Lord, help me stop puking,*
I prayed. *I desperately want to stop.* I pleaded like this every
night, but every new day was more of the same. How was I
ever going to stop this vicious cycle?

I lay in bed that night, my stomach in knots. I'd eaten a
large pizza, a tub of ice cream and cookies; then, I'd purged.
My stomach growled and howled as if a coyote had inhabited my body. It was screaming "No!" from the torture I was
putting it through. On that night and the nights to follow, I
begged and pleaded with myself not to purge, but to no avail.
Night after night, when my parents went to bed, I headed to
the kitchen to grab my "forbidden" food and take it downstairs
to start my ritual.

Cookies, ice cream, cakes, pizza, sugary cereals, and
breakfast bars were my items of choice: any food that I typically wouldn't allow myself to eat, I would crave, give in, then
throw up. In a trance-like state, I would sit on the couch and
down food as quickly as possible while still savoring it all the
way down. My belly would swell to the size of a six-month-
pregnant woman's before it was time for my gag reflex to give
in and dispel the contents. During the eating trance, my mind
would tell me "Feed me, feed me, feed me. Satiate me, satiate
me, yes, fill me up." I felt a sick sort of high consuming large
amounts of food. The initial purging felt like a release—not
only was it a relief to extrude that much food out of my body,
but also to release the tension and anxiety that had built in me

from typical, daily stress. The low came afterward when the physical symptoms of torturing myself began.

Bulimia started after my long battle with anorexia. When my weight went up to over 130 again, I panicked. The weight had come on after a successful breast augmentation. My mother had promised plastic surgery if I recovered from anorexia. From an early age, I had begged her for a breast enhancement. She never even considered saying yes until she felt it was her last resort to encourage me to have a healthy body image. She thought (as well as I) that if I had larger breasts, I would feel better about myself for sure. I had always had a larger bottom, and breast enhancement would complement and balance my body shape. In August of my sophomore year, we chose a doctor who would perform the surgery during my Christmas break.

With the surgery, I went from a AA to a robust DDD. As I woke from the anesthesia, I felt like I had bricks on my chest. My breathing felt heavy as my chest accommodated two fluid-filled sacks. It felt like an elephant had climbed on my chest and nestled into my bosom. I wasn't expecting the rawness of the pain. Neither had I considered what recovery would entail. The surgery required four weeks of almost complete bed rest. Not being active and eating what mom provided allowed me to gain another healthy five pounds. Almost a year after surviving anorexia, I was now twenty pounds heavier.

But to me, the scale seemed to mock me.

What was intended to bring a booster to my image backfired. Larger breasts made me feel bigger, and the weight I gained during recovery propelled me full force into another eating disorder. My brain went into overdrive thinking of ways to get the excess weight off. Anorexia seemed too hard. Since I had learned to actually enjoy food again, I couldn't imagine restricting myself. Exercise felt too difficult due to my newer, bigger breast size. What was I going to do?

My first attempt at purging started one evening after I'd consumed a huge batch of pasta bake. My mother made the best baked pasta with alfredo sauce and pepperoni—delish. But I had taken in way too much, and felt my belly swollen and big. Lying in bed, uncomfortable, I decided to go to the bathroom to attempt throwing it up. It was an immediate success. I had an undeniable, quick gag reflex, and the food came up in one big pile. *Whew.* I felt so much better having the bloated feeling gone. *That wasn't so bad*, I thought. When I went back to bed, I wasn't thinking to myself, *This is it: I've found my new weight loss method.* But from then on, when I ate too much, I'd wait till my parents went to bed and tiptoe to the downstairs bathroom to purge.

So it began, and I started seeing my weight go down. After just a few weeks of my newfound habit, the scales showed an incremental, noticeable difference. The nights of purging became a ritual. To an addict, ritual fuels addictive behavior. Every night, I would eat a tremendous amount of food at the dinner table. My mom was so pleased I was eating. Of course, she didn't realize what was going on after she and my stepfather went to bed.

It wasn't long before I was also consuming and purging large amounts of food during the day. Between college classes, I would come home and enjoy my forbidden foods, then purge, cleanse my face and go back to afternoon classes. This time of day was excellent for hiding my habit. Both my parents were at work, so I had the house to myself to use any one of the four toilets. I usually stayed with the one downstairs because it was my secret toilet, my ritual toilet.

At my deepest, darkest low, I was throwing up four to five times a day. At night after dinner, I would throw up that meal, go for more sweet snacks and throw them up, too. For years, I had denied myself sweets. Discovering I could enjoy them for a moment and then get rid of them was a menacing delight.

My weird behaviors continued and grew worse for two years. Large amounts of money that could have been used for things like new clothes, handbags, shoes, and nights out with friends—which I loved—were being wasted on groceries that were simply being flushed down the commode. I oddly wished my mom had taken notice sooner and asked about the stench in the downstairs bathroom from rotting food particles under the toilet seat that hadn't been cleaned up. I thought she would mention the amount of food I was eating while never gaining an ounce. After I recovered from anorexia, which she was sure I was going to die from, she probably didn't want to say any-thing about me eating too much. My habits had to have seemed a little unusual; I secretly wished someone had brought them up and talked about them with me sooner—though who knows how I would have reacted then.

One morning, after Mom had finished her usual Satur-day morning cleaning, she approached me with the question, "Have you been throwing up? I noticed a horrible smell in your bathroom and saw some dried stuff on the toilet seat."

This was the moment I secretly hoped for, I should have fessed up immediately because I desperately needed help, but I wasn't really ready to face giving up my addiction.

With any addiction, there are three stages. First is the acting out stage, second the recognition stage, and third the bottoming out stage, when one seeks help. I was well on my way to the third stage of wanting help, but was too embarrassed to admit it. Stages one and two quickly passed, and secretly hiding my behaviors was no longer a thrill for me. Eating large quantities of forbidden food stopped being enjoyable. I acted on the behavior because the ritual was deeply embedded in my brain; it begged for more and more. I had my chance to come forward to my mom and seek help, but I didn't. I continued on.

College graduation was rapidly approaching, and I promised myself once I graduated, I would graduate from my eating disorders. I was done. I was moving onto a new phase in my life that would no longer represent the old me. I would use that date as a marker, just like I had used the enticement of a breast enhancement to signal the end of anorexia.

***

It was a joyful time celebrating being the first in my immediate family to receive a college diploma. Neither of my parents graduated from college, so it was a big deal to them and also to me. Mom had sacrificed for years to be able to send me to the college of my choice, and her hard work had paid off. I was finally ready to enter the adult world.

So I thought... The saying, "Wherever you go, there you are," is the absolute truth. Until a significant change is made in the self, no change in geography can decrease the magnitude of help a person needs to overcome a battle within.

The accomplishment of graduating and knowing I had a career awaiting me in the field I desired satisfied me. Life was running its course, and I eagerly awaited the prize. Three months after receiving my BS in Business, I received an offer to manage a dental territory in the greater Atlanta area. My dream from freshman year was to move there and live amongst a thriving community of like-minded people. Moving as far away as I could from the small-town mentality I grew up in was my main goal. The allure of big city life with all the lights, the shopping, the culinary delights, and the hustle and bustle made my soul want to burst into song. I knew I would finally have the platform to make something of myself.

My high ambition, combined with a lack of work experience in the field, caused performance anxiety. Without a foundation of skills, how was I supposed to accomplish the goals set before me? The career I chose came with high stakes: I had a large list of accounts, a 300-mile radius to cover, and a catalog of products to memorize—I had to know the exact features and benefits of each. I had just two weeks of sales training with the company and was then expected to execute growth.

As if moving wasn't stressful enough, I was miles away from home. I couldn't just have mom come over and cook a meal, do my laundry or help me in any way. My freak-out gear went into high alert. I had learned little about functioning on my own in a new city, far from help.

My anxiety manifested full throttle bulimia. Through bulimia, I felt I gained some control. My need for control stemmed from my lack of skills in other areas and doubt that I could succeed. I lacked confidence that I had what it took to handle holding a full-time, pressure-cooker job and paying my high rent.

I had no close friends to help me work through the hardships. I was alone and lonely. But I had become friends with vodka tonics in college and found their friendship soothing.

The perfect storm was brewing. I feared I didn't have what it would take to succeed. There was the pressure of job expectations to meet or exceed my sales quotas. There was laundry, grocery shopping, and taking care of an apartment. My anxiety mounted, panic took over, and the grip of addiction was more out of control than ever. At 22, I could put on a mask and appear to function highly after a night of binge eating, purging, then drinking a few drinks on an empty stomach till I passed out. I'd sleep, wake up, put on a smile, professionally dress, and pound the pavement for dollars.

The saying "You may escape your environment, but you can't escape yourself" is true. That is exactly what happened. Sure, I had escaped the small town and familiarity I had grown up in. Unfortunately, I did not escape the behaviors, addictions, and wrong thought patterns about who I really was. Those came with me. I was out of my league and alone in my new world, and I drank even more.

It didn't take long to find a man who suited the role of a drinking and smoking buddy. It didn't take long to get acquainted with the local liquor store and convenience store where I purchased my daily pack of cigarettes. It didn't take long to find a toilet in my new studio apartment to purge the food I was too scared to digest.

Drunken Affairs

I can pinpoint the time in my life when my love affair with alcohol started. I was newly married. My husband, Daniel, and I had gone to the liquor store to stock our bar with winter-friendly cocktail ingredients: I vividly remember purchasing Frangelica, Kahlua, Yeagermeister, vodka, and rum that evening. It was fun for a little while, having tasty cocktails as my husband and I sat on our front porch in our tiny apartment overlooking Atlanta's gorgeous downtown skyline. We would sit outside, talking for hours, smoking and drinking. It became a nighttime ritual we both enjoyed. I never viewed my drinking or smoking as a problem then. It was controlled, never in excess. It was a way for us to relax and connect as a couple after a long, hard day's work.

The holidays came and passed, and my husband and I continued visiting the liquor store to restock the bar. Soon we became regulars, and the owners knew us by name. I still didn't view drinking as a problem. We were functioning. Work was fine, our marriage was great, and my health wasn't suffering.

Another year went by. In the summer of '07, I hit rock bottom with what I now admit was another addiction. My first husband was in a rock band, and he had come home from practice one evening to have a few cocktails with me. We were out on our back porch in our new house. He had

gone in to refill his cup when I blacked out. I fell backward, thankfully on a chair. I hit my head hard, and I didn't
remember what had happened. Daniel told me what had
happened afterward while I lay on the couch with an ice
pack on my head. That was the first of two blackouts I experienced that summer.

During this period, I started developing a panic disorder. At
first, I had no idea what was going on with my body. My first
experience with a panic attack made me think I was having a
heart attack. My heart viciously palpated, my head swam, I
felt dizzy, and my hands tingled and went numb. I was driving
west on I-20, going to make routine sales calls, when it began.
The white lines separating lanes seemed to sway, moving back
and forth as dizziness consumed my vision. I pulled off the
interstate and called Daniel. He advised me to go to the local
hospital immediately.

I safely executed the drive a few miles back into the city to
the local hospital. In the ER, they performed routine blood and
urine testing. The pregnancy test was negative, and the EKG
evaluation was normal. Every test came back negative, so they
let me change back into my clothes and discharged me. Maybe
I was going crazy—nothing was physically wrong with me. I
went home early that day from work and rested. Maybe I was
stressed, and that's what brought it on. I look back now and
realize I didn't put two and two together: drinking was taking
a toll on my neurological system.

Over the next few months, the panic attacks became more
frequent and severe. My life, and especially my work, started
suffering. The most severe panic attack I had was in a sales

meeting with a client. We were discussing the portfolio of products when I went into one of my episodes. My legs went weak, my heart raced, my thoughts vacillated between the conversation I was having with the dentist and my own inner, agitated dialogue. I backed up a few steps to balance myself against the wall, trying to concentrate on what we were talking about and avoid going limp and passing out. I eventually had to excuse myself from the meeting and drove to a Doc in the Box near my house.

This was the first time I received a clear diagnosis. The doctor asked me a few questions and quickly concluded that I was experiencing panic attacks. He wrote me a prescription for an anti-anxiety medication and sent me on my way. I had it filled immediately so I could start getting in the medication in my system. Before taking my first dose, I read the back of the bottle: "Do not take with alcohol." I wanted to feel better physically, but take away my alcohol? No, thank you. I stored the pills in the medicine cabinet. I would not take them till I was ready to quit drinking.

***

Another few months passed. I was in complete denial of my drinking problem. Though I recognized I had a problem, I felt trapped in myself, and I didn't know how to quit, how to break free, or what it would take to stop the cycle. However, I decided to start the medication that the Doc in the Box had prescribed. I thought I would give it a try—yes, with alcohol, yes despite the warning—to see if it would alleviate my constant anxiety and stress. However, the medication—combined with my high alcohol consumption—made matters worse.

Two weeks later, I sat in the chair at my psychotherapist's office. Nervous and on the brink of a nervous breakdown, afraid to speak about my emotions, I cautiously responded to her questions. Question after question, answer after answer, we slowly started peeling back the layers of past experiences I had subconsciously buried and not dealt with. After an hour of evaluation, she diagnosed me with post-traumatic stress syndrome (PTSD).

I had never realized the powerful effect of my father's neglect on my self-esteem and the relationships I later developed with men. My feelings of rejection led to internalized anger and self-destructive behaviors. Our discussion led to the state of my marriage and living as a co-dependent alcoholic. There was a lot of baggage that I needed to sort out before I could establish a healthy dose of serotonin in my brain. My main goal was to be able to concentrate and function without panic attacks interrupting my days.

Daniel's drinking continued to worsen, he began to cocoon into his own shell, and his ability to love me vanished. As the months came and went, we grew further apart. Daniel and I began living as roommates. The chasm between us grew deeper, although my craving for intimacy and longing to be accepted never waned.

I started an affair in the fall of 2009 on an internet site, and it was the final straw that eroded any potential for our reconciliation. The man I met online, Cal, would penetrate the deepest longings of my innermost being and get the deepest cravings of my soul through the emails we exchanged. He wooed me with glittery words, his voice and his deep, passionate intellect. He was the one I'd been craving; he finally "got" me. I could feel my soul rejoicing. I could feel my heart palpitating again that someone could cherish me as a human being and care enough to share and participate in my life instead of merely getting drunk together. Need and immaturity outweighed the voice of my grown inner adult, which said this affair was a very bad idea.

I knew this was bad: he was married, I was married, he had kids and a family, and Daniel needed me. But I was so charmed. I was caught in a web of being wanted, feeling needed and cherished. Cal and I exchanged countless emails and phone calls. Our marriages were unfulfilling and distant; we were avoided, unappreciated and discounted. Within our affair, we sought affirmation and love.

***

Fast forward to June 2010. I had enrolled in cosmetology school in Atlanta after losing my position as a territory account manager. I took a short break and went to visit my mother in North Carolina. While I was visiting, a phone call came from Daniel at home.

Extreme profanities blasted my ear. "I can't believe you. Again?"

There was nothing I could do but hold up my hands in surrender and say, "Yes, I did it again." This was in fact my third emotional affair outside of our marriage.

There were email trails, phone calls, and trips to visit that were now in the open. There was no denying or excusing it away. I'd been exposed, and I couldn't ignore it. I had to face the shameful truth. I wanted to blame Daniel for forcing me into the arms of another man. If it hadn't been for his alcoholic behavior, we wouldn't be where we were.

I remember the ride back to my Atlanta home. I smoked cigarettes like a freight train, not knowing how Daniel would act when I arrived. I knew I had gone too far. I made a fateful assumption, there was no hope for a future with Daniel.

I met with the divorce attorney a few days later to go over the distribution of assets, the normal dispersal between the two failed parties of a marriage. We went over the affair and whether Daniel had legal rights to more than I did because of my personal failings in the marriage. At that moment, I was clueless about what was going on. I thought I was just being freed from Daniel's alcoholism.

But such pride I had! What I was being released to was more of my own behaviors and more of trying to fill my neediness through men. Do you think Cal broke it off with his wife because I was going through a divorce? Of course not! I felt like a fool as his demeanor toward me became mockingly empathetic.

But the divorce papers were drawn, and a large sum of money was paid toward the debt our separation caused. I decided to move back to North Carolina. In order not to lose the credit hours I'd earned in cosmetology school in Atlanta,

I asked for a curriculum transfer to continue my education in North Carolina.

***

Three weeks after beginning school again, I received a phone call that rocked my world. I was on the top floor of the parking deck. The voice on the other end pierced my ears, stopped my heartbeat, and threw me into a panic like I had never known before.

Daniel was dead.

My husband was dead. He had hung himself on our back porch.

I screamed, *Why?* I sobbed as time stood still.

My shriek reverberated around the half-empty lot. I remember a man, a doppelgänger of the lead singer of AC/DC, standing on the top step of the landing. He looked at me in sheer terror, wondering what was going on.

I ran past him, down the flights of stairs into the school. I announced to whoever was there, "Daniel's dead."

A few teachers consoled me the best they could, but they didn't know what to do other than have me fill out a request form for two weeks' leave.

I had just filed a request for two weeks' leave prior to transferring schools, and now I had to request another for a death in the family.

***

The drive down to my house with my father was long and painful, silent and numbing. I was still pseudo-talking to

Cal. He had experienced the suicidal death of a friend in high school, and from that experience, offered his condolences as best as he could. I tried not to blame Cal or myself for Daniel's death. But I did feel I was to blame as the cause of Daniel's suicide. *If it wasn't for me, he would still be alive. If it wasn't for my affairs, he would still be here.* Then I got angry. *If it wasn't for his alcohol, he would still be here.* Thoughts came and went. Blames and shames would come to haunt me, and then, reason would come and go.

The rest of my family arrived the following day. All pitched in and packed up the house. In a day, I'd lost my husband and my home. My father called around to several real estate agents and had the house listed by a woman who promised to have it sold sooner rather than later. But after three months of an outstanding mortgage balance, I decided the only thing I could do financially was let the house go into foreclosure.

Following Daniel's death, many toxic relationships ensued. There was a girl from school who persuaded me I couldn't function with the opposite sex because I was truly a lesbian. There was a second marriage to an immigrant who needed me for a green card. Then, a second divorce after just four months of marriage and the realization that I couldn't support a man on my meager income as a newly-licensed cosmetologist. I had numerous encounters and escapades resulting from exchanges through a dating website—including meeting my now-husband.

Bill saw right through my provocative behaviors into the wounded child behind the pretense of glitz and glam. Even though my triggers triggered him and vice-versa, I knew he didn't only desire me for a brief escapade or a few casual encounters. He wanted me for the long haul, the journey of ups and downs, the around-abouts, through the wastelands and the wilderness. He knew beauty was ahead, beckoning me forward. Neither of us knew we were en route to a crash collision with Jesus. The upward calling of Christ was coming.

PART TWO

Note to the Reader:

Days turned into weeks and then into months of a ravenous love affair with the Word of God. The glory so deeply impressed upon my soul from my bathroom encounter had wrecked any appearance of what had been "normal" in my life. I woke to read the Word, I took breaks between clients to immerse myself in study, and on the nights Bill and I didn't go on dates, I saturated myself in the Bible, in worship or listening to a pastor teach on YouTube. I had never heard the word "revival" to describe my experience, but I was 100% being revived by the Spirit of the Living God, taking off the "old man" and replacing it with a new self, created to be like God, in true righteousness and holiness (Ephesians 4:24).

There was a shift in my earthly desires of what I wore, how I talked, and who I wanted to surround myself with. The first area the Holy Spirit began working on in me was clothing. Marshalls was my favorite place to shop. I was known to frequent the store on new shipment days and was often one of the first shoppers to preview the new offerings. I have fond memories of Holy Spirit's nudge to hand over that desire. I obeyed. I felt Him urging me: "For a complete year, I don't want you to touch foot in here." The hunch to lay down my shopping habit was strong, and I didn't want to disobey my first love's voice. The year cycled through as I yielded to wearing only what was in my closet. Only once did I have to shop, and it was due to an unexpected temperature drop while I was out with Bill on a date one night—I didn't have a coat. I felt the Holy Spirit blessing me with an opportunity to pick up a coat on clearance so I wouldn't freeze.

I threw out provocative, low cut, cleavage-bearing tops and exchanged them for full-coverage ones. Tight pants revealing my runner's physique were exchanged for looser fitting garments. A full face of makeup, earrings, necklaces, bracelets also beckoned at the altar. On my way to work in the morning, I would worship. In those times, I encountered the Father's heart towards me, and I would break out in tears. I would have to sit in my car and redo my makeup before entering the building. This became too much of a chore, so I stopped wearing eye liner and mascara. I felt too worldly wearing fashion jewelry and accessories, so those, too, were surrendered. High heels were traded for flats. My bright red mohawk underwent transformation into a longer blonde bob. The red felt rebellious, the blonde softer and subtle. As the Lord was tenderizing my heart, I was changing outwardly.

The Holy Spirit had a finger on my mouth, how I spoke and what I said—mainly concerning how much profanity I used to convey strong emotions in conversation. He had me research adjectives as descriptives for how I felt so I could better express myself and communicate a strong sense so that my speech assertively clarified my feelings. (A bottle of Tums became my close friend as I stewarded halting my use of profane words when I was upset.)

My friend group changed completely. I actually wanted friends—I didn't want to live like a lone ranger. I sought out friendships with those also seeking the Lord. I had zero sense of what Christian life looked like since I had been away from that way of life for so long. I wanted fellowship with believers who were under the conviction and direction of the Holy Spirit, not those focused on religious works. I prayed and prayed for God to show me where to find women of faith. He opened the door for me to join a home study fellowship just minutes down the road from church. This group of ladies were like none I had ever experienced before. They were filled with fire for the Lord, they had gifts of prophecy, healing, tongues, prophetic singing, visions and prayer. I left each week so grateful to God for giving me this opportunity to see His hand clearly at work in my desires to get to know Him deeper through operating in others. There was so much more than I could have ever imagined available to me through Christ and fellowship with His Holy Spirit.

As mentioned in Chapter 1, during this time of breaking and breakthrough, the Spirit took me back to the Garden of Eden where it all began to impart deep truths about who I was, according to God, to help me understand how I got to where I was, and to begin the deep work of becoming a new creation in Him. As I dug deep into the scripture, I began journaling the revelations of profound truth that were breaking up the fallow ground of the garden of my heart, growing and solidifying faith in its place.

Here is where I want to take you by the hand into the transformation chambers of the Word that changed me in hope that these same truths will ignite in you a holy desire and passion to know Christ, the hope of your glory, in a new and fresh way.

So, in Part Two, while I will share a few more stories from my life, mostly, I want to share what I've learned about God through scripture and fellowship with Him. I hope that through my descriptions and reflections, you can too grow closer to God or begin a relationship with Him if you've never had one. If you have experienced disappointment or trauma, depression, addiction, or been without hope, my prayer is that my story and the story of God's love for us all inspires you to follow Him.

Chapter 6—

MADE IN HIS IMAGE

So God created humans to be like himself; he made men and women. God gave them his blessing and said: Have a lot of children! Fill the earth with people and bring it under your control. Rule over the fish in the ocean, the birds in the sky, and every animal on the earth. (Genesis 1:26–28, CEV)

H e made humans in His image.
Blessed them.
Gave them authority and dominion.

As the Lord took me back to consider the beginning in the Garden, where He made Adam and Eve, He began opening my eyes to His original intent for humankind. Words like *image, blessing,* and *dominion* leaped off the page of the life-giving Word into my spirit. They spoke directly into the dark night of my soul, engaging the lies that left me barren, broken and hopeless. The truth was God made me with passion and purpose. "And God looked upon all that He had made, and indeed, it was very good" (Genesis 1:31, BSB). There was a clear intention in creation: I was good, I was pleasing to God. He loved me, and I, in turn, was given access to love Him back.

I began to see God as creator and parent, both a good Father and nurturing Mother. I saw His dual qualities of lion and lamb: He's fierce but meek, softly woos yet strongly protects. He was taking me back to the drawing board of who He framed me to be when I was formed in my mother's womb so I could catch the revelation and begin rebuilding my life around the image of my destiny in Christ. I was created not for another human's agenda nor others' opinions of who I should or ought to be. I was created with a purpose and plan and given the inherent qualities needed to carry them out with Him. This realization initiated my chase to pursue God and discover who that woman really was.

You, too, were made in the image of God. What an honor! What a privilege! What a weight of responsibility. Out of all of God's creation, He wanted us to share in His likeness: His ways, His will, and His governmental authority. To rule and reign over the earth, the birds in the air, the fish in the sea and every living creature. God's original intent was for us to reign over the earth as He reigns over heaven. He purposed our creation to be creators with Him. He blessed us with abilities to function as He functions.

We were created to be the channels of His divine orchestration to keep order here on earth as in heaven. As He drew me in deeper with His Word, the more intimately He revealed what this actually means. I'm still on the journey of knowing, but I do know it begins with prayer. He drew me into understanding the importance and power of praying the scripture. I began reading books about becoming a prayer warrior. I learned about the influence I have in intercessory prayer. Through it, we partner with God and see His kingdom expand as we speak with Him about areas that need His divine breakthrough. After all, it was through the spoken word of God that He framed the world (Psalm 33:9).

He blessed us! His ultimate design was for us to live in perfect communion and unadulterated intimacy with Him forever. Our bodies wouldn't wear out and decay; immortality would be our portion. When Adam and Eve were created and walked with God in the Garden of Eden, they were naked. I believe they weren't only physically naked but internally naked, and they had no shame. Everything in them was exposed and laid bare: there was no shame because they were enveloped in the glory of God.

He designed us for partnership through marriage with children as offspring: hence, He created both genders with the ability to procreate through intimacy. He designed us to have fellowship with others and Him to fulfill our deepest needs to belong and feel significance and purpose. He knew the deepest longings of our hearts were to be pursued, affirmed in love, safe and intimately known—naked without shame.

We were hewn together by His purposed intention, for we are His workmanship, created in Christ Jesus for good works, which God prepared beforehand, that we should walk in them (Ephesians 2:10). Unlike any other animal God created, we are unique in that we have capacities patterned after those of our creator. For instance, any time you deduce something through logic and use reason to find a solution to a problem, you are functioning in the likeness of God, for He is strategic and thoughtful.

There are many names ascribed to God in His word to denote his character and attributes. God (*El Elohim*) is the Creator. He created the sun and the moon, the stars in the sky, the heavens and earth, people, plants and animals. Anytime you create something using your hands, whether through painting, welding, sculpting, or building, you operate in this attribute of God. Anytime you get bothered by the cruelness of society, children being bullied, or racist slurs boil your blood, you are being bothered by the moral compass of God (*Elohei Mishpat*) in you. God is a God who supplies (*Jehovah Jireh*). Anytime you make a friend, take a meal to a new mom, a neighbor that just returned home from surgery, visit a shut-in, or serve at your local homeless shelter, you are operating in the image of God. All of these great attributes of God are all nestled within us. Even if we haven't activated them, they are part of our DNA, ready to be activated and carried out.

Another attribute God gave us was free will. In His great love for us, God created us with the ability to choose. Choice establishes free will. We have the autonomy to make decisions. Choice affords us a life that doesn't feel like we're puppets walking around on marionette strings, with every action orchestrated by someone other than ourselves. Without choice, life would feel contrived and mundane, controlled and manipulated. By and through choice, we have free will to operate with God or separately from Him.

He gives us choice because He's not a tyrant. He's not on a power trip. He doesn't need to run us around and tell us what to do to puff Himself up. He is God, and He doesn't need us to do anything. If He wanted to, He could do whatever He wished. But He says from a heart of love, "I want you to have authority, I want you to have rule and say so." But with that authority comes the responsibility to choose wisely.

I set this up with the sobering reality that we don't always choose wisely. We enjoy the autonomy to function in the abilities God has given us, without considering Him. We choose our own way, function outside God's established government, and become our own gods. Yes: we can function as our own gods because God has given us those abilities. But if we don't stay under His sovereignty, we fall into self-orbit. God's anointing recedes, and we are left to function on our own.

Let me explain by going back to the Garden of Eden.

The LORD God took the man and put him in the Garden of Eden to work it and take care of it. And the Lord God commanded the man, "You are free to eat from any tree in the garden; but

you must not eat from the tree of the knowledge of good and evil, for when you eat from it
you will certainly die."
(Genesis 2:15–17, NIV)

By setting two trees—the tree of knowledge of good and evil and the tree of life—in the garden, God laid the foundation for choice. Adam and Eve's ability to choose was established, and the consequences for choosing wrongly were clearly stated. Within the garden of perfection, there was only one thing they should not choose. They could take advantage of anything except that one thing—the tree of the knowledge of good and evil.

If there is an ability to choose, there is equally a consequence for the choices one makes. Consequences are the result or effect of an action or condition. For Adam and Eve, the consequence for their choice was death. When God created the choice, its consequence showed the significance of the weight of that choice. He paired the highest consequence, death, with a choice He forewarned them not to make.

If God loved them, why would He create choices that led to clearly negative consequences? It was to show the value of His love. *Value* is "the regard that something is held to deserve; the importance, worth, or usefulness of something." Its synonyms are *worth, advantage, benefit, gain, profit,* and *merit.* The value of His love establishes worth, importance, usefulness, and merit. Adam and Eve had access to the highest value of love in existence—walking in perfect communion with God.

The repercussion of partaking in the fruit from the forbidden tree was death. The consequence matched the value of the relationship with the Lord. God's consequence showed a clear value for the result of disobedience: death. It was death that had the power to separate man from God in holiness. Holiness, in its essence, cannot commune with unholiness; it's a law of purity. In setting this precedent, God knew that if they chose to disobey and partake of the fruit, they would be split apart from their intimate bond with Him. In no way does God ever want us to choose a life separate from Him, but He has to allow it because love allows choice.

Adam and Eve exercised their ability to choose, ate fruit from the tree they were told not to and were banished from the once fairytale-like habitation, Eden. A close look into the garden gives us insight into what we do today. When Adam and Eve made their choice, it gave rule and dominion to the darkness of this world. For God said, "Eat it and surely you will die." This death would prove to be a spiritual death that disconnected humanity from the Father. The Spirit would be ripped from us, and we would be left in a body with our own limitations apart from the empowerment of the creator, God. Generations from Adam onward fell into this curse, and the rulers, powers and principalities of the world now ruled over them.

When Adam sinned, the entire world was affected. Sin entered human experience, and death was the result. And so death followed this sin, casting its shadow over all humanity, because all have sinned.
(Romans 5:12, TPT)

When sin entered the world, it was through one man. In essence, *sin* is missing the mark. What is the mark? It is holiness. After the sin of Adam and Eve, the generations that followed were marked with this dreadful disease. Murder, envy, jealousy, drunkenness, incest and more sins sprung forth out of Adam and Eve's bloodline. One man's disobedience caused the entire lineage of his offspring to be under chastisement. Humanity was now banished from the garden and set apart in their own land to work and toil using their own strength. As separate entities from God, they would now have to work hard, strive to earn the fruit of labor and make blood sacrifices for sin just to enter into God's presence. He warned they would die, but it wasn't just physical death: it was also internal. Adam might have wished he was physically dead because the work and toil that went into living apart from God was hard.

Life apart from Christ looks similar. When we are disconnected from His mercy and grace, striving becomes our close ally. It is a natural overflow from a lack of grace. In our own efforts, life is summed up by *doing* instead of *being*. The focus is on self-effort. *What can I do? How can I make things right?* Self-sufficiency says, "I have to *do* in order to *be*." You protect the self, and you provide for the self. You labor in vain for the self. It's exhausting! You live under the curse and don't even know it. The curse sent the wages of death and living life apart from God. Being caught in an endless cycle of doing and performing to find favor in this life is exhausting.

After the fall, the requirements to reestablish a relationship with God came with their own consequences. Since death resulted from sin, God required an offering of blood in the form of animal sacrifice to enter His holiness. Why blood? Blood gives life to things, and blood cleanses and purifies. Life would have to be sacrificed as payment for sin for people to receive forgiveness. So animal sacrifice was instituted, and the blood of the most prized animal out of the herd was to lay on the altar in atonement for sin.

Through Moses, the old covenant explains how animal sacrifice allowed us into God's presence. However, there was a greater sacrifice to come that would be sufficient for all time. There would be a permanent closure to death. Before the foundation of the world, God had in mind His only son Jesus to be the perfect lamb, the spotless sacrifice to take away sin forever. Jesus came to earth over 2,000 years ago and lived a perfect life in submission to the Father in order to be the atoning lamb of mercy. His blood would be sufficient once and for all to restore the sons and daughters to the Father God. Through God's grace and mercy, Jesus provided a way and made it possible to restore mankind to Him through the perfect sacrifice: Jesus on the cross. This restoration allows us to function as the image bearers of God, co-creating with God, reigning and ruling with God and enjoying the beauty of His Presence.

Let's journey forward into the details of the fall and glean wisdom on how to be restored once and for all to God our Father through our Lord Jesus Christ.

Chapter 7—

THE WORLD'S SEDUCTION

The thief comes only to steal and kill and destroy. I have come that they have life, and have it to the full. (John 10:10, NIV)

God created the Garden of Eden as a utopia for Adam and Eve where they could have perfect communion with their creator and one another. They were given the opportunity to grow, prosper, reign and have dominion over that territory. One thing God didn't tell them was that the craftiest of all beasts roamed around in this land, too. This beast was clever and prudent. He carefully articulated his words; he was calculated and shrewd. He strategically used seemingly sensible intelligence, which infused confusion in his prey. Through his disarming devices, he sought to inject doubt into God's truth and sought to label Him as a liar. The beast asked questions to dismantle the clarity of God's truth. The best deceivers are not those who speak mistruth but those who call truth into question.

> **Do I understand that God told you not to eat from any tree in the garden? (Genesis 3:1, MSG)**

I want to delve into the exchange between the deceiver and the couple to see how the conversation began. Then, we can extrapolate how the enemy's tactics are still used against us today.

First, there is a clarification question. The serpent asks, "Any tree?" In doing so, he encompasses all trees instead of one. Why? Did he actually know which tree, or did he want them to point it out? Was he using an opening line just to begin a conversation?

Unlike God, the enemy isn't omniscient (all-knowing). He only knows bits and pieces. He needs us to fill in the blanks. So, he asks for clarification that gives evidence, which he then uses to support his means by twisting and thwarting it.

The enemy can only operate effectively if we take his bait and begin to doubt the truth. In general, questions do just that: they provoke us to examine our beliefs. Do we believe what we've been told? Do we accept what is? The greatest form of manipulation can be exerted by getting us to question the truth. This is powerful because it has the potential to unground us in our convictions by shaking the roots of our core beliefs.

The more ungrounded we are in the truth, the more vulnerable we are to having it taken away. Think about it: if we are not 100% convinced, questioning can sow further doubts. Therefore, the truth must be an impermeable reality in our hearts so that deception cannot pervert what is planted. Jesus' parable of the sower speaks to this point. Jesus relates His Word to seeds and connects how a seed is planted within our hearts to determine how it will affect our inward parts.

I was brought up in a Christian home. Sundays and Wednesdays were set aside for church activities. Nights were spent doing devotions before bed, and prayers were the norm around the dinner table. The name of Jesus wasn't withheld from my upbringing. I grew up in church under the moral conviction of what was God and what wasn't. It wasn't just about what was right and wrong—though that was part of it—the question was, "Is it good or God? Is it faith or fear?". The religion I was brought up in was good, but it didn't have the active ingredient that awed me and made me curious for more of the height, the depth, and the breadth of God. I didn't see the movement of the Holy Spirit. I only felt the weight of religion (the religious spirit, if you will) and a legalistic set of rules I was to obey. Because awe at the wonder of God wasn't an integral part of my church experience, I fell away at the bait of temptation. The groups of parties seemed to be free, seemed to be having fun, seemed to have it all, or so I thought. I didn't see people getting wild and having fun in fellowship with God: they seemed uptight and rigid. I wanted fun and a good time.

The deception of the world outside of church lured me into a lifestyle that snowballed into a stronghold of sin.

College came; I was introduced to higher learning. Courses that made me question my beliefs were standard in my field of studies, business, at a liberal arts school. Since I wasn't completely rooted in my faith, I was easily persuaded out of my religious doctrine. Other religions, ethics, debate, and philosophy were introduced to my impressionable mind. Going to church and praying shallow prayers was about as spiritual as I was. Not having a personal relationship with Jesus allowed me to be swayed by all I was learning. I was a prime target, easily led astray by "higher thinking" and conceptualism. These dogmas or higher conscious philosophies piqued my interest. I thought I found wisdom above what I had been exposed to in church. This new realm of thought struck a chord in me. From college into my twenties, the study of New Age philosophy, Buddhism, Daoism, and higher conscious awareness bloomed in my soul. Through meditation, yoga, and chanting, I felt like I was connecting to a higher power. But as my brain expanded, my soul was still trapped in darkness. I struggled with my self-concept; I struggled with alcohol and cigarettes; I struggled with anxiety and depression. All the things the world religions said they would offer me—to empty my mind, free my soul, and attract positivity through gratitude—didn't do a thing at all. I began to feel foolish for even thinking that they could.

The world had crept in and corrupted the planted seed of the Word I had learned as a youth. As the Lord led me to study the enemy and his tactics, it was easy to see how being a novice in Christianity and not a devoted believer led me straight into the enemy's trap.

In the Parable of the Sower, Jesus goes into depth outlining what happens when God's truth isn't planted in a heart of faith.

> **A farmer went out to sow his seed. As he was scattering the seed, some fell along the path, and the birds came and ate it up. Some fell on rocky places, where it did not have much soil. It sprang up quickly, because the soil was shallow. But when the sun came up, the plants were scorched, and they withered because they had no root. Other seed fell among thorns, which grew up and choked the plants. Still other seed fell on good soil, where it produced a crop—a hundred, sixty or thirty times what was sown. Whoever has ears, let them hear.**
> **(Matthew 13:3–9, NIV)**

How the seed is sown is important to the crop it yields. The Word, sown into our hearts, can fall away. Therefore, we must guard our hearts and what we allow in and around us so that God's Word isn't snatched away, uprooted, stolen, or killed. We can overcome any obstacle by remaining in His Word, meditating, and applying faith to whatever challenge we are walking through. Remaining in and meditating on His Word means that we discipline ourselves to keep a regular habit of reading and thinking about what is said to us over and over. Remember, the thief comes to steal, kill, and destroy. That is the Word of God. However, if we are properly rooted and grounded in the Word, the Word will work out life abundantly in our situations. If we remain in Him and meditate when trials come, we have a lifeline from which to work.

I had certainly not remained in God's Word. It wasn't fully planted, and the cares and sorrows of this world uprooted it from my heart. Seeds of doubt and distrust were sown and took root, and I had completely fallen away. Yet, God drew me back into His fold.

One of the ways He drew me was through conversation with my inner man. What exactly is the inner man? The inner man is the location within our spirit that the Holy Spirit, which you receive when you accept Jesus into your heart, lives and communes within us. We are three-part beings: body, soul, and spirit. Our physical bodies are what you can see, our soul is comprised of our mind, will, and emotions, and our spirit is the part of ourselves that is unique in that God uses that channel of His Spirit to communicate with us (or other spirits if you aren't currently a believer in Christ). We commune with God, and He with us, through the Holy Spirit. This is effectively what prayer is. In the inner chamber in our hearts, we intercede, communicate with, and make supplications to God. This is also where we receive revelation when we read the Word of God. This is why the Word is powerful and active because it discerns the thoughts, intentions and motivations of the heart.

Moreover, I will give you a new heart and put a new spirit within you; and I will remove the

heart of stone from your flesh and give you a heart of flesh. I will put My Spirit within you and cause you to walk in My statutes, and you will be careful to observe My ordinances. (Ezekiel 36:26–27, NASB)

In Christian therapy, I learned to hear and discern the voice of God speaking, activating my inner man. (If you would like more information on how to personally hear from the Lord, Mark Virkler's *Four Keys to Hearing from God* is the best resource.) The more you are in the Word of God, thinking and meditating on it, the more Holy Spirit will reveal Himself to you. I found the Holy Spirit's greatest activity when I was running while listening to worship music through my iPod. He had my full attention on the roads since I was alone and focused on Him. One morning while running, the Lord spoke to my inner heart while I was on turning onto Bethel Drive. (The word *Bethel* is significant all by itself. If you want to read more about it, you can find it in the book of Genesis, where Jacob encounters the Lord for the first time on the stairwell to heaven.) "What does the cross mean to you?" the Spirit asked me. I was in shock. I replied, "First, Lord, seriously, I know you died on a cross, and you shed your blood for me on that day—but why are you asking that?"

As I kept running up the long, winding hill of Bethel, I realized why God had asked me that question. He knew I knew of the cross but asked if my heart knew the reality of what had happened there. He hung naked with people mocking Him; He was tortured, literally tortured, and became sin and felt the weight of our sin upon Him. He felt a disconnection from the Father so intense that he cried out, "Father, why have you forsaken me?" He felt the weight of being disconnected from the only source of comfort and connection. This was one of the first times in my Christian walk I felt Him tenderly pulling at my heartstrings.

I began to understand the lengths my savior went to to help me see love in its fullest expression. He helped me understand that I don't have to do my life alone, that He sees and loves me, that He cares about me, He died for me. Not only did He die, but He did it in the most undignified way, on a cross, naked. In ancient history, being hung on a cross was the worst penalty. The Word says, "Cursed is everyone who hanged on a tree" (Deuteronomy 21:23) because, under Mosaic law, those who died this way were cursed. His love wanted me to understand the cross, not because He was challenging my intellect but my relationship with Him and my heart toward that reality. He was challenging my "truth"—my internal truth of who Jesus is. Was He real to me? Did His sacrifice do anything in my heart that would reveal my acceptance in Him and my true identity as His child?

When God provoked this conversation in my heart, it was a truly humbling experience. I've played that time over and over again in my head, rehashing it until it became a "Bethel experience" for me, a moment in time when God showed up and revealed the truth of who He is to me, my Savior, one who understands and deeply cares. He was beginning to plant His Word by revelation so deeply that truths of His heart would flourish in mine.

Listen then to what the parable of the sower means: When anyone hears the message about the kingdom and does not understand it, the evil one comes and snatches away what was sown in their heart. This is the seed sown along the path. The seed falling on rocky ground refers to someone who hears the word and at once receives it with joy. But since they have no root, they last only a short time. When trouble or persecution comes because of the word, they quickly fall away. The seed falling among the thorns refers to someone who hears the word, but the worries of this life and the deceitfulness of wealth choke the word, making it unfruitful. But the seed falling on good soil refers to someone who hears the word and understands it. This is the one who produces a crop, yielding a hundred, sixty or thirty times what was sown. (Matthew 13:18–23, NIV)

We see here in one of Jesus's parables that *seed* refers to the Word that has been heard. If it's not understood, it will be quickly snatched from our hearts. *Understanding* here refers to personal application of wisdom through the revealed Word of God. The seed can produce joy for a time but quickly slip away when trouble comes. We love to believe the Word until we are tested. The Word is good news until we have to walk by faith and not sight, meaning we have to believe what God says in His Word over the facts and feelings of a particular situation. The seed can be choked out by the worries and cares of this world. They seem to overshadow the truth of God's Word, so we need faith to override feelings and worries. The seed planted in the one who hears, understands, and obeys is seed that produces a crop. That seed yields more than what was sown. In simple terms, this means that the Word "taught but not caught" cannot yield change or a harvest.

For years, I never understood the Word of God. It was a religious duty for me to attend church, but my Spirit wasn't in a position to receive the Word because I wasn't born again of the Spirit of God. One of the Holy Spirit's responsibilities is revealing the Word of God with understanding—like when I was running, and the Holy Spirit revealed the importance of the cross.

> **For the message of the cross is foolishness to those who are perishing, but to us who are being saved it is the power of God. For it is written: "I will destroy the wisdom of the wise; the intelligence of the intelligent I will frustrate."**
> **(1 Corinthians 1:18, NIV)**

A seed has to be planted, and it must take root. Once the seed finds good soil in our hearts, it has to remain there. What is good soil for that seed to fall into? Good soil is a heart that has been prepared for the good news of the gospel. The heart needs to be fertile ground for anything to grow well. A farmer knows that for a seed to do well, its environment has to be well-irrigated, tilled, fertilized and planted deeply enough that storms don't uproot the plant that grows from it. Our hearts are the soil a seed goes down into. The well-watered ground is like how well we water our hearts with the living water of the Word. Are we spending time in His Word? Are we meditating on who He is and who we are in Him? Are we allowing His truths to permeate us and remove the lies we've believed?

The living water comes so that we can nurture a root system in Him that grows to be an oak of righteousness. Oak trees are the oldest tree on the planet and existed before humans. The Word says we are oaks of righteousness planted by living streams of water. Since oaks have a huge root system that reaches for water to survive, we, too, need to be planted closely to God's Word and reach for it daily so we can survive the elements of this harsh world. Then we can grow to be firm, strong and solid like the firmly planted oak.

The second element in growing good seed is tilling the land to cultivate a proper environment for the seed to grow. I used to watch my grandmother till the soil in her garden each spring before she planted new seeds. I always wondered why, but I never asked. I just knew it needed to be done. Upon researching, I learned that tilling, or cultivating, the soil removes weeds from the garden because it brings their roots to the surface where the sun will scorch them. It also loosens the soil and thus optimizes the soil's retention of air, water and nutrients where the new seed will be planted.

This cultivating process is similar in our hearts. The weeds are unforgiveness, anger, bitterness, envy, jealousy, contempt and pride. With these weeds in our garden, a new seed doesn't have much ground to take root in. By the grace of the Holy

Spirit working in us, we must uproot sin in our hearts. As we allow the tilling of the Holy Spirit to search and know us and any offense or wicked way in our hearts, we allow what is unnecessary and helpful to be brought to the surface and burned by the fire of God. The Lord then has room to replace unrighteousness with righteousness: His living water (the Word), His air (in Hebrew, *ruach*, or breath of heaven). The nutrients of love, joy, peace, patience, faithfulness, gentleness, kindness, and self-control can take root where the weeds once lived.

This garden within our hearts is truly supernatural. It's amazing how the Holy Spirit works in the darkness of our inner man. As we spend time in God's Word, He recreates us from the inside out. The ability of His Word to cut through spirit and soul tends to these weeds of sin as we read the Word, study it, and allow what it says to affect us. When we allow the Gardener of our hearts to do what He does best, to cut out dead places in us, we have good ground for this seed of God to take root and be deeply planted in us. So when the enemy comes, and he will surely come, we have a deeply rooted implantation of who God is and who we are in Him that the enemy can't quickly tear away. Our firm foundation on which to stand is quickened in us so that it won't be stolen by suggestion. It won't be stolen when hardship comes. It won't be stolen when disease comes. It allows us to be strong when we suddenly lose a job, a loved one dies, a marriage crumbles, or we are tempted by the riches of this world. We will know without a doubt that the Lord is our rich reward, and His Word is more true than what the world can offer.

This is foundational to our walk with the Lord. If we allow deceit to steal what God implants in us by His Word, the enemy will come in and seduce us into believing lies.

The Word is a powerful weapon against deceit. Take what you are up against and say, "Well, the Lord says in His Word that this is my reality and these two don't line up, so I'm going to believe the Word over what I see." That's when we activate faith.

Faith is the substance of things hoped for, the evidence of things not yet seen.
(Hebrews 11:1, KJV)

Faith comes by hearing, and hearing by the word of God.
(Romans 10:17, NKJV)

Let me break this down.

Faith is believing, not seeing. It's believing God's Word over what you see with your natural eyes. Faith is a gift from God. This winter my daughter introduced me to the movie *Polar Express*. At the end of the movie, a bell from one of Santa's reindeer is misplaced. When the little boy awakes Christmas morning, it reappears under the Christmas tree. It contains a letter which explains that if you Believe, you can hear the bell ring. Oh, how I delighted in this illustration which metaphorically describes the activation of our faith. We hope for things not seen, but it is believing that activates the power of God in our lives. The activation power of faith comes when we receive and trust that Jesus is the Son of God who lived, died, and was resurrected, and we invite Him into our hearts. Faith is the highway from which we bring heaven to earth in us. When we are born again, we experience the transference of giving us to Him and Him to us.

I used faith in overcoming my addiction. These were a few of my fighting verses:

> **Do not get drunk on wine, which leads to reckless indiscretion. Instead, be filled with the Spirit. (Ephesians 5:18, BSB)**

> **Wine is a mocker, strong drink is a brawler, and whoever is led astray by it is not wise.**
> **(Proverbs 20:1, NKJV)**

> **We all experience times of testing... But God will be faithful to you. He will screen and filter the severity, nature, and timing of every test or trial you face so that you can bear it. And each test is an opportunity to trust him more, for along with every trial, God had provided for you a way of escape that will bring you out of it victoriously.**
> **(1 Corinthians 10:13, TPT)**

I used these verses in prayer to put a demand on heaven, that by faith I would inherit the power generated through the Holy Spirit to break the stronghold this substance had over my mind and life. I taped the verses on walls I saw frequently. I put them in my bathroom and in an area in my bedroom where I could read and meditate on God's Word. I needed to remind myself I could conquer this trap, that God would provide a way to lead me out of temptation, and that I needed to be filled with the power of the Holy Spirit instead of wine.

Mind you, I had never felt like a conqueror. I felt victimized my whole life. I had always given in to temptation. I never felt like I had a choice, so I chose poorly. Wine—not the Spirit—became my way of escape. I would pray and plead, *Father, deliver me from wine, from the need to escape. Please deliver me from wanting this and desiring this. This is too strong for me.*

My prayer was much like David's prayer:

> **Even though I was helpless in the hands**
> **of my hateful, strong enemy,**
> **you were good to deliver me.**
> **When I was at my weakest, my enemies attacked—**
> **but the Lord held on to me.**
> **His love broke open the way**
> **and he brought me into a beautiful broad place**
> **He rescued me—because his delight is in me!**
> **(Psalm 18:17–19, TPT)**

I was helpless when I tried to quit drinking alcohol. Its lure was too strong for me to walk away from on my own. I was a puppet in its grip. My lack of ability to regulate myself and stop strong emotions from tidal waving over me anytime sadness, doubt, confusion, depression, and anxiety crept in meant alcohol's numbing properties overpowered me. The Lord knew I needed His strong arm and grip to hold me and carry me away from this enemy that tormented me daily.

I cried out daily in prayer for deliverance. I repeated in my head, *I am an overcomer: the Lord is going to offer a way out of temptation and help me walk in the power of the Spirit, not the power of wine.* Faith that God would do what He said He would do helped me practice patience while I waited for Him to strengthen me in this battle.

God desires to set us free, to deliver us from chains and bondage, and He knows the best way to lead us. He strengthens and empowers us inwardly so we can be equipped with the knowledge, understanding and application of His Word to be mighty warriors. But, you might be wondering, if God is good, why doesn't He just deliver us? Why do we have to battle? Why doesn't He just take the pain away? Why wouldn't He miraculously deliver everyone who asked from addiction?

Everyone's story with the Lord is unique. Often, He will use a problem to create a relationship so that He can show you His character, love and grace. If I had been instantly delivered from my addictions, I wouldn't have formed a deep relationship with Him through prayer and studying His Word. By pursuing Him intimately, I was equipped with what I needed to strengthen myself, regulate my emotions, and be delivered from a victim mentality. He aligned my mind with His truth so that I could easily discern lies and choose to walk in the light of His righteousness. Through seeking Him, His Word, and His truth daily, my mind was rewired. When my mind became aligned with the power of the Word of God, I began seeing results in my efforts to abstain from drinking.

In the next chapter, I will describe another activation of faith for the impartation of deliverance.

Chapter 8—

TWISTED TRUTH

The woman said to the serpent, "We may eat fruit from the trees in the garden, but God did say, 'You must not eat fruit from the tree that is in the middle of the garden, and you must not touch it, or you will die.'" "You will not certainly die," the serpent said to the woman. "For God knows that when you eat from it your eyes will be opened, and you will be like God, knowing good and evil."
(Genesis 3:2–5, NIV)

E ve offered valuable information to the serpent which he twisted and used against her. She pointed out the exact tree in question that God said not to partake of, giving the serpent the opportunity to add his spin to God's word.

This exchange opened my eyes to examine who and what I allowed access into my life. Who I engage in conversation with matters. What I listen to matters. Too much information provided to the wrong person can allow the enemy access into our lives, and he can then pervert, twist and distort what God wants to plant in us. The enemy used a snake then, and he can use whoever and whatever to devise schemes against us now (TV, internet, phone, books or other people) to gain access into our hearts and minds. His main goal is to get us to question the absolute truth of God's Word and authority in our lives.

"For we are not fighting against flesh-and-blood enemies, but against evil rulers and authorities of the unseen world, against mighty powers in this dark world, and against evil spirits in the heavenly places" (Ephesians 6:12, NLT).

The war has already been won, but we are to be warriors of faith contending for what is rightfully ours in Christ now. The enemy still prowls around, hoping that the Word of Christ hasn't taken root in our hearts, that we haven't gained a true understanding of the gospel or that the worries and cares of this world will choke out the Word, or that trouble and persecution make us fall away.

If we don't stand firm on the promises of God, and with our full armor on (Ephesians 6:13–17) the enemy comes in and plunders what we have. For it to take root in our hearts, we have to know what the Word says. With it, we can resist the subtle tactics of the enemy and live victoriously. One of the gifts of the Holy Spirit, spiritual discernment, aids us in identifying the enemy's shrewd tactics. This blessed gift helps us discern the spirit by which someone or something operates from.

> **Beloved, do not believe every spirit, but test the spirits to determine if they are from God, because many false prophets have gone out into the world.**
> **(1 John 4:1, NKJV).**

We are called to test and approve what is of God and what isn't. *To test* means to:

— examine,
— prove, and
— scrutinize.

These are active words. It is our active duty to see that what we learn, see and hear aligns with the Word of God. We are encouraged to do so because there is only one way to God, and that is through Jesus. Every other door is illegitimate and leads to death and destruction of our soul and spirit. Doors represent openings. Here in the natural world, doors open to new places, homes, and rooms. In the spirit, doors are open by other religions, false teachings, philosophies, New Age practices, the occult, necromancy (communicating with the dead), mediums, and psychics to name a few. They are also opened by fear, hatred/unforgiveness, and sexual sin.

In my journey and quest to know Jesus and be filled with more of His love, I was made aware of the enemy and his devices though a book I was given, *New Age Cults & Religions*, written by Texe Mares. Within this 337-page book, many different cults and religions were listed—false ways and forms of seeking God that lead others away from the gospel truth. I was shocked to realize I had participated in seeking truth from a variety of these religions. Buddhism, Doaism, New Age, A Course in Miracles all opened doors to the enemy to twist and pervert the truth of God's Word. They were ways to the god of this age, but not the only way to the One, True, Living God which is Christ Jesus. I am not the only one who has been tripped up by other teachings in finding the way to God. Once I discovered these entryways, it was my duty to close them and abandon their false teachings, throw away the books away and repent to the Lord.

Once I did thorough inventory and identified all the doors I had opened, my Christian therapist led me in a series of prayers to seek forgiveness, renunciation of my participation in opening those doors, and asking Jesus to close the doors and seal them with His blood. (If you would like further information, *The Bondage Breaker* by Neil Anderson is a thorough resource to identify areas in your life where the enemy may be using deception against you.)

Deception in the Church

Prior to receiving *New Age Cults & Religions*, I was awakened one night to a dream regarding this subject. I believe it was not only a warning for me but for others who are young in Christ. One of the gifts the Lord has provided me is the gift of dreams. I dream several dreams a night, and they often contain prophetic insights. I take these dreams very seriously because since God communicated to His people in dreams in the Word, I know He still does the same today (Acts 2:7, Joel 2:28, Daniel 1:17).

In this dream, I was a bystander at an outdoor children's play. Children frolicked around the stage, enjoying the theme of the play, which involved a lion. Suddenly, a real lion appeared from behind the stage. It pounced into the crowd. With several ferocious bites, it gobbled up children while the parents stood in horror. As I watched, a fierceness rose in me. All of these innocent, beautiful babes—devoured because of a reckless mishap! I stood amongst the bloodshed and cried out.

I shared the dream with a friend later that day. Her interpretation was that the children represented those young in Christ or unaware of salvation. The lion represented the enemy. He comes out from nowhere, behind the curtains in life, and devours innocent, unknowing ones. This revelation stirred a fire in my bones. We must be aware! We must be sober and alert, the Word says, for "the devil prowls around like a roaring lion, seeking someone to devour" (1 Peter 5:8, NASB).

The enemy is described in the Word as: the *prince of the power of the air* (Ephesians 2:2). *Prince* refers to power he has. *Air* refers to the invisible realm where he rules the present darkness of this age. This spirit works in those who are disobedient to God. He desires worshipers just like God and will tempt anyone in any clever way he can. He parades around like an angel of light (2 Corinthians 11:14). He masks himself as an archetype of love, power, goodness and truth in order to tempt, persuade and seduce unaware people into his kingdom. I know this firsthand. Since I wasn't persuaded by my Christian upbringing that Christ was the only way to God, I became fascinated and overcome with the magical mysticism of other religions that seemed to be peaceful, harmonious and loving. It was the way that seemed right to me, but I was clearly deceived.

Satan's goal was and still is to have followers just like God does. Because he is jealous of God's power and authority, he seeks to gain followers using conversation as his bait. *Did God really say that? Do you really believe Him?* He operates in our thinking: *I know what's best. God didn't really mean that, did He?* We take the bait of the enemy's devices when we don't believe what God said and turn to others or ourselves for our own "truth," or truth apart from the Gospel.

As he did with Eve, he questions God's authority of and calls Him a liar. In conversation with Eve, the serpent said, "You will certainly not die.... For God knows that when you eat from it your eyes will be opened, and you will be like God, knowing good and evil" (Genesis 3:4–5, NIV). But she was already like God! God made Eve in His image. So how could she believe the serpent's lie?

Why would the enemy set the couple up? Why would he misrepresent God's command against them? Because he wanted to be like God. He had tried and failed miserably. In his boasting attempts, he was cast to earth along with one-third of the other rebellious angels.

> How you are fallen from heaven, O Lucifer, son of the morning! How you are cut down to the ground, you who weakened the nations! For you have said in your heart: "I will ascend into heaven, I will exalt my throne above the stars of God; I will also sit on the mount of the congregation on the farthest sides of the north; I will ascend above the heights of the clouds, I will be like the Most High."
> (Isaiah 14:12–14, ESV)

Notice how many times the phrase "I will" is mentioned. Lucifer precedes each statement of his assertion with, "I will." Pride was Satan's downfall. He wanted to be like God and function as his own god. Instead, God cast him out of heaven and lowered him here to earth. Satan projected his own desires onto Eve to reel her into what he wanted. Through this cleverness, he got Eve to question God.

When we question God, when we allow the enemy to twist and pervert God's truth. We allow earthly, demonic and sensual messages to reframe the holiness of God's pure Word. Sadly, in a lot of churches today hyper-grace messages excuse sin and propagate prosperity over the full authority of God. We don't need a gospel that excuses sin but one that delivers us from it. No one that truly has met Jesus keeps on sinning.

All who indulge in a sinful life are dangerously lawless, for sin is a major disruption of God's order. Surely you know that Christ showed up in order to get rid of sin. There is no sin in him, and sin is not part of his program. No one who lives deeply in Christ makes a practice of sin. None of those who do practice sin have taken a good look at Christ. They've got him all backward.
(1 John 3:4–6, MSG)

When I accepted Christ in my life and began seeking Him daily and diligently, I could begin to see another spirit begin to work in me: the Holy Spirit.

Now we have not received the spirit of this world, but the Spirit who is from God, that we might understand the things freely given us by God.
(1 Corinthians 2:12, ESV)

The Holy Spirit is the spirit of holiness driven by righteousness (right standing with God and man), peace, love and joy. When I came to know Christ in a personal way, I didn't want to keep on sinning. I wanted to know and fellowship with Jesus who overcame the power of this world. When I read the Word and was convicted of sin, I longed to be set free of it, asking in prayer for the Holy Spirit to help me overcome it. I knew I was powerless in and of myself to change since for so many years I had no power to change. I stood in awe and wonder of what

Jesus did for me on the cross, and that revelation gave me the faith to believe that with the power of His Spirit living within me, I could overcome sin that had had me in its grips for too long. I had counted the cost to follow Him and that was what provoked my daily desires.

Deception Within Ourselves

You were once in darkness, but now you are in the light in the Lord, so live your life as children of the light. Light produces fruit that consists of every sort of goodness, justice, and truth. Therefore, test everything to see what's pleasing to the Lord, and don't participate in the unfruitful actions of darkness. Instead, you should reveal the truth about them.
(Ephesians 5:8–11, CEB)

Here again, we see the word *test*. In this context, test means to allow, discern, examine, approve and try. We are told to test what is pleasing to the Lord and not to participate in unfruitful actions of darkness.

What does darkness look like? It is disobedience to God, His Word, His will, and His way. Living by the carnal flesh is one way. The "flesh" is comprised of our mind, will and desires. In following the flesh, we will be driven by envy, lust, lying, bitterness, jealousy, anger, and being overly critical, to name a few. A flesh-driven person will desire and covet control and power, and they will operate out of rebellion and idolatry.

When I was unsaved, life was all about me. I focused on getting my way, meeting my needs, living out of my own resources (my thoughts, opinions, reasonings, education, looks, talents and abilities). I was envious, I would lie to get my way, and I manipulated others to make sure situations were favorable to me. I was bitter and critical of those I was jealous of. I had partnered with the enemy's lies of rejection, abandonment and accusation. I was living a life less than what Christ died to give me.

The truth of the Gospel exposed these fruitless deeds of darkness and gave me the power to cut through demonic lies. I was neither rejected nor abandoned. The Spirit of adoption had sealed me as a child of the King, and I wasn't left alone to figure out life as a vagabond. Everything I needed to live life wisely was located in God's Word. I didn't need to be my own god and figure out life by myself. I needed the Gospel truth with its power to save me from myself and the bondage of this world. I repented and exchanged what I felt and believed for the truth.

God's truth has the power to transform us and to make us whole again. This truth must become our confession. When we speak the Word of truth, it is our weapon of righteousness against the kingdom of darkness. There is power in our words. Our words give us the ability to create life or death. When we speak the truth and the Word, authority resides on those sound waves and accomplishes what we speak. As the Lord created, He spoke the world into existence. At the command of His voice, the heavens and earth were created. Everything living and breathing contains an echo of the essence of God. We contain that very breath, the *ruach*, the existence of God within us. So when we declare His blessings over us, the earthly powers that have us bound are loosed by the authority our words carry.

How did this look for me? When negative chatter would begin in my head—*you are a reject; you aren't wanted; you aren't worthy; you will never do that, achieve this*, and so on and so on—I would go to a mirror, look at myself, and confess scripture. At first, I felt like a fraud because I was so conditioned to repeat and believe negative lies about myself. It became an exercise of patience and perseverance as I kept repeating scripture about being loved and belonging until I actually felt the confession as truth.

When I began to criticize another person, I took a look within and asked myself if that person made me feel insecure or jealous. If the answer was yes, I would respond in prayer, something like this: *Father, I feel insecure around this person, and I know it's because I am jealous. I don't want to be jealous. I want to enjoy success with them. I want to lift them up and not feel insecure because they are soaring in life. I know if I confess my sin to You, You are faithful and just to forgive me of my sin and make me new.*

The Father is faithful! He began to grow my heart for others I had once felt insecure or jealous around. Instead of standing on the sidelines with a critical attitude, I was able to wholeheartedly applaud their success. I knew it was the grace of God to allow me to do so because comparison and competition had clouded my vision for so long. It is amazing what God can do with a contrite and humble heart before Him (Psalm 51:17).

Defeating Alcohol Once and For All

Knowing the Word helps us be clear-minded and sober. In God's Word, *clear-minded* represents clarity. *Sober* refers to being calm and collected in spirit.

> **The end of all things is at hand; therefore be self-controlled and sober-minded for the sake of your prayers.**
> **(1 Peter 4:7, ESV)**

I desired to be clear-minded: to think and see clearly. I longed to be sober and sober-minded.

I was tired of using wine to calm my nerves and believing the lie that it did. I wanted to think clearly.

> **Don't get drunk on wine, which produces depravity. Instead be filled with the Spirit in the following ways: speak to each other with psalms, hymns, and spiritual songs; sing and make music to the Lord in your hearts.**
> **(Ephesians 5:18–19, CEB)**

I can speak from experience that wine never made me have good judgment. I felt it freed me from fear and insecurity because my defenses were down, but this twisted lie never calmed me. No, it made me weak and open to vulnerability.

I fought this lie with the Word day after day after day until the Word felt like truth in my inner being and allowed deliverance. In the heat of the battle, I remember driving home from church one day, really wanting to win my battle with alcohol. I no longer wanted to crave or desire it. I had come a long, long way in my recovery and in renewing my mind in the Word of God, but I still hadn't gained victory over strong drink. I was still drawn to a nightly relaxation routine which included alcohol.

One evening in church, we studied the power of our words. We identified lies that empowered negative behaviors and re-aligned ourselves with gospel truth. Lies that kept me tied to drinking behavior became clear to me. While worshipping in my car on the way home, the lies started whispering what they wanted me to believe. As each one appeared, I started verbally renouncing them:

— You are not my comfort.
— You are not my reward.
— You are not my friend.
— You are not my safety.
— You don't make me brave.
— You are not my confidence.
— You don't satisfy me.
— You don't empower me.

As I started renouncing what alcohol had told me over the years, tears poured from my eyes. I wept over the lies alcohol had used to bind me to it. All the things alcohol had falsely promised were supposed to be why I loved Jesus. Wasn't He my comfort, my reward, my friend, my safety, my courage, my confidence, my satisfaction and the one that empowered me to do great things? I immediately started praying, "I'm sorry, Father. Please forgive me for believing these lies. Jesus, You are all these things and more to me." That night, my soul was saved.

In my own strength, I had been able to abstain from alcohol for almost a year. However, the craving and the desire had never left. Though I could refuse a beverage, the taste still came to my lips, and the longing would bubble to the surface. A holy frustration set me on a path for full deliverance. I wanted complete freedom since that is what the Word of God says is available to me: who the Son sets free is free indeed (John 8:36). By faith, from the message I received that night, and as led by the Holy Spirit, I spoke truth to the lies the spirit of alcohol tempted me with. When I renounced what alcohol made me feel, I knew the grace of heaven had punched the lies that had inhibited my freedom and released deliverance into my soul. I knew this time, I was truly free because the desire immediately left.

A car later whizzed by me with the license plate, "Granted." I knew without a shadow of a doubt that I was delivered. Thank you, Holy Spirit!

Chapter 9—

BARGAINING AGAINST TRUTH

When the woman saw that the fruit of the tree was good for food and pleasing to the eye, also desirable for gaining wisdom, she took some and ate it. She also gave some to her husband, who was with her, and he ate it.
(Genesis 3:6, NIV)

E ve saw the fruit of the tree was: 1) good for her flesh, 2) appealed to her eye and 3) desirable for wisdom, and she ate it.

> **For everything in the world—the lust of the flesh, the lust of the eyes, and the pride of life—comes not from the Father but from the world. (1 John 2:16, NIV)**

What tempts us to sin? In First John, we see the three things that tempted Eve, and they are the same that tempt us now. It pleases our flesh, it looks good, and it will somehow allow us to achieve higher enlightenment than what we already have, the pride of life.

The lust of the flesh is any desire in excess of normal appetites toward anything the body naturally needs. For example, the body needs food, but overeating for pleasure causes an unhealthy imbalance. The reverse—a lack of food, starving the body—is harsh treatment of the vessel we are called to take care of.

Nowadays food is treated as an art form and an indulgence. But it was meant to be fuel, a source of energy for our body, not an indulgence for sensual pleasure. When it's artfully prepared, beautiful cuisine can create an absolutely amazing experience. I am guilty of glorifying food; I love expensive food. I've been taken to several dinners that cost over 500 dollars! I felt so fancy eating artisanal food; the feelings were very real.

Yet, how ignorant I was to tie my worth to food! I really didn't want to hear about it at first, but the Lord started teaching me: "The kingdom of God does not consist of food and drink, but righteousness, peace and joy in the Holy Spirit" (Romans 14:17, NET). I felt a deep conviction that He wanted to work on my appetites. It wasn't necessarily that my expensive taste was bad. But food was made for the body, not the body for food. God wanted to break my persuasion that going out to dinner and choosing the best wine pairings was a necessity: it was nice, but it was a luxury and not something that led to abundant living. Just because I enjoyed fine food and wine, they could never define who I am. So while I still have the freedom to enjoy them, they are no longer a priority. (I needed this revelation if for no other reason than that my bank account did not support my expensive palate.) I was seeking His kingdom and righteousness first. So, since He said I was mistaken in my ways of seeking Him, I knew laying aside that sensual pleasure would allow fulfillment of promises I really needed: peace and joy in the Holy Spirit.

No pricey meal will ever equate to peace and joy in the Holy Spirit. As we grow in the discipline of obedience, laying down earthly pursuits and surrendering our fleshly desires to the Spirit, we can carry the gift of heaven in us as we were designed to from the beginning. The kingdom of heaven really is here if we follow the Spirit's lead.

***

Sexual desire is also considered lust of the flesh. Sex was designed to seal the covenant between a married couple. When a woman has sex the first time, her hymen is broken, which causes a flow of blood, therefore creating a covenant. This covenant is like the one we have with Jesus: it is the seal of being set apart. When we set ourselves apart to our spouses through the covenant of sexual intercourse, we create a bond that God said was good and is for us to enjoy. However, outside the marriage covenant, sex exposes the body to weakness.

> **Run from sexual sin! No other sin so clearly affects the body as this one does. For sexual immorality is a sin against your own body.**
> **(1 Corinthians 6:18, NLT)**

In our society, the loss of virginity is touted as a rite of passage. It's as acceptable as eating and drinking. However, as seen in the Word, we sin against our own body when we commit any act of sexual immorality, including sex outside of marriage covenant.

Statistically, those who have had many sexual partners or have been sexually abused have higher rates of depression, low self-esteem, and more suicidal ideation. When we commit sexual sin, or it has been committed against us, we begin to hate the very body we are told to care for. Self-loathing, self-hatred, and body confusion are overflows of sexual sin.

I mentioned my entry into the world of sex through an unwanted sexual encounter. That experience opened a door to a perverted perception of how I should attract males. Yes, I was abused, but in a weird, twisted way, I thought to have any guy's attention I must be physically intimate. It is sad to admit the truth, but after a few years of promiscuity, I identified with the term "maneater." I was fueled by the lust of men who would give me attention if I gave them something in bed.

In the attempt to feel worthwhile, I threw my worth away into the arms of guy after guy, hoping to receive the love and affirmation I longed for. However, the pain of shame ate away at me, and as it did, my confidence eroded. With this mind-set, I inadvertently invited more substitutes to try and fill the emptiness and void within myself, including alcohol and cigarettes, anorexia and bulimia. I remember being convicted of my sexual sin over and over before I met the Lord. I would get in the shower hoping to scrub away all the filth I felt from promiscuity. I cried aloud as I scoured my body with soap, but nothing could wash away my sin till I found out how the blood of Jesus did.

In Christian therapy sessions, I learned how to effectively apply the cleansing blood of Jesus to my sexual sin through prayer and renunciation of sexual relationships. These helped break the soul ties that spiritually bound me to previous partners. When we sin against our bodies through sex, we give away part of our soul to another person. Through sex, we create a bond that allows a partner access into us and us into that partner. To break that bond, we need to prayerfully un-partner ourselves, which effectively closes the door the enemy uses to torment the soul. When we do, we release the soul tie that attaches us to the other in the realm of the spirit.

For me, it took verbally renouncing my participation with them, asking for forgiveness, sending back to them the parts I stole, and asking the Lord to bring back all that I gave from myself. By the Holy Spirit's grace, I took back all the parts of me that were stolen, misplaced, and abused—mainly innocence, purity and a chaste perspective of intimacy.

Maybe you recognize soul ties you made with others in the past, and maybe you want to be free from them. You've given your body away, sacrificing beautiful parts of yourself in order to feel some sort of acceptance, a false love. Perhaps that's left you feeling less than worthy and unclean.

If you have been a victim of physical assault, rape, incest, or molestation, my heart goes out to you. All are horrible offenses. As hard as it is to forgive (I know it personally), it is vital to take this step of faith toward your offender for *you*. Forgiveness is always for your benefit. It releases the debt the other owes you. It allows the Lord's justice to proceed and for Him to fight the battle to renew and heal you.

In my recovery from sexual promiscuity, I recognized the entry point of lust occurred when I was raped. As hard as it was to forgive the rapist who violated me, I had to. I couldn't do it, though, without asking for the Lord to help. In my own strength, I simply couldn't.

I cried out: "Lord, you forgave me when I didn't know what I was doing. Please help me forgive him. Please heal and restore my mind, my body and my emotions from this trauma, this abuse against my body. Release back to me the parts of my innocence, purity, integrity, beauty, and childhood that were stolen that night. Fight for me, defend me and take back what the enemy tried to steal from me. I send all parts back to him that were given to me through this sexual encounter. Demon of lust, you must go in Jesus' name; I send you back to your owner. Come fill me, Jesus, with Your sanctifying blood and fill me, Holy Spirit with Your revelation light of purity, justification, and sanctification. I need Your love, purity, and peace to flood every part of me that's been mistreated and abused."

The Lord did exactly that. He flooded me with His love, and He will flood you with His love. He wants His beloved children restored to a place of purity and holy passion for His name. He wants to fight and defend the things that have been lost, stolen and dead in your life. He is the Father of life, and He promises to restore and give life abundantly to those who seek Him.

If this is you and you would like to pray a prayer to restore sexual purity, repeat this prayer out loud:

> *Father God, I thank you for saving me from destruction. I praise you for sending Jesus to die for my sins. Please forgive me for my sins against you. Specifically, I confess that I _____ (details of the sin). I repent of those sins and renounce it now. Lord, please purify my heart from this sin, the memory of it and any associated fantasy I have entertained in my mind regarding it. In the name of Jesus Christ and by the power of his blood shed on the cross, I cut myself free from any soul ties that may have been established with _____ (name (s) or specific objects). I commit him/her/ them to the care of Jesus Christ for him to do with as he wills. Satan, I rebuke you in all your works and ways. I rebuke any evil spirits that have a foothold in me. In the name of Jesus, I command you evil spirits to leave me and go directly to Jesus Christ. Father, please heal my*

soul of any wounds resulting from these soul ties. Please reintegrate any part of me that may have been detained through this/these soul ties and restore me to wholeness. I also ask that you will reintegrate any part of the person(s) I sinned with that has been detained in me, and restore them to wholeness. Thank you, Lord, for your healing power and your perfect love for me. May I glorify you with my life from this point forward. In Jesus' name, Amen.
(From "Prayer to Cut Soul Ties," Missionaries Of Prayer, January 21, 2021, https://www.missionariesofprayer.org/2010/11/prayer-cut-soul-ties/)

Lust of the Eye

Eve saw the fruit was pleasing to the eye and partook of its pleasure
(Genesis 3:6 NIV).

Perception is everything. Perception is the ability to see, hear, or become aware of something through the senses. The eye is used to see, and how we see is very important. When we have an eye examination, our physical, perceptive vision is measured. Are we far-sighted or near-sighted? However, spiritually our perception is related to how well we "see" things, and how we govern our sense of the Lord in everything. When we are born again into the Lord, we receive a new awareness into the things of God. Our sight gains perception of new dimensions in the revelation of Christ. We see beyond the seen into the unseen.

Paul, an apostle of Christ Jesus, had an encounter with the Lord that exemplifies what it means to have one's eyes opened. Paul was a strict Pharisee, a teacher of the Law of Moses. He once persecuted followers of Jesus because his eyes were spiritually blind to the Messiah that had appeared. However, despite this blindness, he encountered Jesus on the road to Damascus. The encounter left him physically blind for three days. On the third day, the Word says that scales fell from his eyes, and he regained his sight. In those three days, the touch from the Lord transposed his spiritual sight from darkness to light. Paul went from persecuting followers of Jesus to leading people to Christ. What did Jesus touch to bring this about? Paul's eyes! Eyes are so important to how we see and perceive things.

> **Your eyes are windows into your body. If you open your eyes wide in wonder and belief, your body fills up with light. If you live squinty-eyed in greed and distrust, your body is a musty cellar. If you pull the blinds on your windows, what a dark life you will have!**
> **(Matthew 6:22–23, MSG)**

The only way to be filled with Christ's light is to be filled with the Spirit of the living God, the One who fills our body with light and who brings us from death to life with just one touch. Scripture exhorts us over and over again to *see* things correctly because temptation can happen through faulty perception. The book of Matthew states:

> **And if your eye causes you to sin, tear it out and throw it away. It is better for you to enter life with one eye than with two eyes to be thrown into the hell of fire.**
> **(Matthew 18:9, ESV)**

As Eve was tempted by what she saw, we see things pleasing to the eye and say, "Well it looks good to me; it must be good." But we must stop and examine whether something is merely good or if it is truly from God. It may look good; it is probably pleasing to the eye; but in the end, it may cost a great deal. We must guard ourselves in this area and ask for God's grace if we find we allow what we see to tempt us into sin. Lust, envy, greed, jealousy, and competition all begin in the eye.

We see what someone else has and we covet or envy it, whether it is a lifestyle or possessions. In Christian circles, we may covet or envy giftings and callings. We think we should have those, too, and jealousy bears witness in our hearts. We get envious of our neighbor who can afford expensive vacations or a Louis Vuitton purse, or who has a loving marriage or children. We compete with one another, and our focus on one-upmanship steals the opportunity for connection and community. The truth is that when we get lost in things of the flesh, we walk away from the commandment to love. We can't love with greed, envy, jealousy, competition, and lust in our eyes. They are at war with love.

Dying to the flesh and coming alive in Christ wins the war. Having the Lord as your reward above all else will work in your heart and He will wage war against envy, jealousy, and lust. We all have unique talents, gifts, and callings He will expose and develop, but that can only happen in the secret place in fellowship with Him. Get alone with Him and let Him begin to teach you who you are. He alone is the one, true authority in your life. He made you: He formed you in your mother's womb. You are fearfully and wonderfully made (Psalm 139:13–14). He longs to establish a relationship where all lies are exposed in the safety of His perfect love as you establish a permanent residence for His genuine affections to nestle deep within.

As a child, I saw the attention my half-sister and stepsister received from my father. The only difference I could see they had, and I did not, was looks. My older half-sister had long, silky brown hair, big boobs and a tiny waist. My younger stepsister had long flowing blonde hair, a cute figure and legs like a model. Me? I was frumpy. My teenage years were awkward. I had frizzy, wiry hair. Before the popularity of flat irons, I would actually lay my head down on the ironing board so my mom could take a clothes iron to my hair to tame the frizz. I carried a lot of weight on my frame, as my genetics allowed me to gain weight easily. I was tall for my age, but not skinny-tall. I was a giant, large-tall. It didn't take much comparison to see I was markedly different than most at my age. All this comparison at a young age and the distance I felt from my father led to my self-loathing and a preoccupation with making myself desirable at any cost. Jealousy, envy, greed, and competition started early for me. I thought: *If I could just be* this *way, I would be accepted. If I could just be a little more* that *way, I would be loved.* Lies that I wasn't good enough, acceptable enough, skinny enough, pretty enough, or smart enough ran like kryptonite through my veins.

By eighteen, I had a full-blown eating disorder. Anorexia gained me the attention I craved. Boys started to notice me more; my dad finally gave me the words of affirmation I so longed to hear. I got a modeling contract with one of the top agencies in my area and was getting bookings. What no one knew was how imprisoned I felt. Sure, I might have looked more conventionally appealing than previously, but the self-hatred it took to fuel that kind of behavior ran rampant in my mind and body. It became a competition between me and the scale to see how low I could go.

What initially led me—jealousy, envy, and competition—had overtaken my life, spun me out of control, and set me on a path for self-destruction of anything positive in my life. Everything I did was the result of trying to find affirmation that I was good enough, worthy enough, and a viable, lovable person. My body had been overtaken with darkness. I had no wonder, no awe. I had become a deep, dank, dark cellar. Sure, I looked appealing on the outside, but inwardly, I was a cavern of emptiness.

Are there areas in your life that have become overrun with competition, envy, jealousy, or greed? Has your eye darkened to the glorious light as you've tried to live up to a standard that you think is the bar of the highest glory? There is no shame here, no need to feel condemnation if yes is your answer. Admit it, tell the Lord your struggles and ask for His mercy, receive His grace, and walk in the anointing of empowering grace to your own destiny, free from comparison.

Desirable for Wisdom

...and also desirable for gaining wisdom, she took some and ate it.
(Genesis 3:6, NIV)

Why would having wisdom be any better than what Adam and Eve already had in the paradise of the Garden of Eden? I don't know. Scripture does not reveal why Eve felt she didn't already have it all. But, on careful reflection into humans as we are, I know we tend to focus on what we don't have rather than what we do have. So, maybe Eve's focus was a little off base. Maybe she stopped focusing on what God surrounded her with, so it seemed to pale in comparison to what she didn't have, simply because she disregarded the importance of God's command.

I don't know if you are already formulating where I am going with this. But to me, when I started studying the fall of humanity, it became clear what God was addressing regarding issues of perceived lack and in turn misunderstanding God's best for us. Let me delve into what I believe He revealed to me.

We enter into conversations with ourselves daily regarding these issues:

— Lust (financial and material wealth, status, position, power, gluttony)
— Greed (the need to handle circumstances and situations to defend ourselves, envy, lack of empathy, manipulation, an overemphasis of needing to have more)
— Coveting (comparison of what others have that you do not)
— Adultery (sexual relationships when at least one partner is married—also, I believe idolatry falls into this category. Idolatry is any way we place our own desires, hopes, ambitions, heart alliances, and affections in place of God in our lives. It also includes our identity and how we want to be seen, whether that be materially, with our job status or physical appearance)
— The world around us—especially that which seems just out of reach—is enticing. It seems to offer something more enriching—or at least more tangible—than pursuing life with the Lord.

We start justifications in our mind: *Did God really tell me to do that? Does the scripture really mean that? If God was so loving, He would just want me to be happy—right?*

We question our parents and people in authority: *Did Mom and Dad really say I shouldn't do that? I know the Bible says wait until marriage to have sex, but this one time won't hurt.*

I know the Bible says He will seek my revenge but I'm going to gossip about this person long enough to try to ruin their character because they deeply hurt me. God says my body is a temple, but I'll quit this addiction tomorrow. I love my spouse, but I'll look at just this one more picture, one more video of this naked woman.

The sense of lack draws us into sin, and many scriptures teach this. Lack is what causes murder, warfare, disharmony, and disunion. "You desire but do not have, so you kill. You covet but you cannot get what you want, so you quarrel and fight. You do not have because you do not ask God" (James 4:2, NIV).

Worldly mindsets believe happiness reigns supreme. You hear, "I just want you to be happy." Happiness is the key to a good life. If it makes you happy, just do it. But if we judge our quality of life by what makes us happy, then we will never get to holiness. Why? Because doing the right thing, according to God's standard, through His Word, doesn't always equate to happiness. Our soul has to learn that obedience isn't always pleasurable. Doing the right thing doesn't always feel good. We are obedient because of our love for God, not because our flesh says, "This feels so awesome."

Does God care that it doesn't feel good? Absolutely! Does God care you are in pain? Absolutely! Does God care that you are down and out? Absolutely. That is why He sent Jesus to fill in the gaps of our dissatisfactions. A relationship with Jesus through the Holy Spirit can be the most rewarding experience. Learning to submit to Him and get in the flow of the river takes time, practice, and the will to allow it to happen.

God cares the most about what you are going through—pain and suffering, waiting, heartache, or loss. He makes all things beautiful in His time (Ecclesiastes 3:11). In waiting, we experience things from God we would never experience if He was a genie in a bottle.

Chapter 10—

SIN LOVES COMPANY

She also gave some to her husband, who was with her, and he ate it. Then the eyes of both of them were opened, and they realized they were naked; so they sewed fig leaves together and made coverings for themselves.
(Genesis 3:6–7 NIV)

Immediately Adam and Eve saw what was going on. They realized they were naked and covered themselves. Their eyes were opened, but not in the sense they perceived. They had hoped for more wisdom but instead received vision that brought shame. Can you imagine how they must have felt? Expecting... then receiving... and what you receive is nothing at all like you expected?

Nine times out of ten, I bet you know exactly how this feels. You do something enticing because you believe the lie: you choose it, believing it will give you something *more*. You are led to believe through your external judgment: *It's not that bad. Just this one time.* Maybe you drank to be more popular, had sex to get the guy/girl you thought you had to have, and bought into a lifestyle that's draining you financially to keep up with those around you. If you've lived life at all, you've probably been deceived into believing one thing and experiencing another.

As Adam and Eve felt shame after disobeying the Father, I'm sure you have, too. Going against truth leaves us feeling bare and naked—not in a physical sense, of course, but in the reality that our vulnerability is exposed. We feel it at our deepest core—our identity. We are created with an internal sense of good and evil. It's in our nature to feel the consequence of sin. The consequence usually pierces right to the heart where we're convicted that what we've done is wrong.

Can you separate who you are from what you did? Can you separate what was done to you to see who you are? The inability to do that produces a shame mentality. Shame makes you feel ugly, dirty, unclean, and unkempt. The sins I mentioned previously, the "one-time" deals, can start to pile offense on top of offense to the inner self. Shame then damages the very core and essence of who you were created to be.

The leaves we use to cover and protect ourselves are uncomfortable and inhibit how we relate to ourselves, others, and God. This barrier to intimacy hinders your ability to be real with others and creates chameleon-esque behaviors. The thought of being transparent makes us uncomfortable. Out of the overflow of not feeling good enough, we put on a mask and create a false self to function in this world. The word *personality* actually means *mask*. Our personality reflects our mask. Are you the funny one? The serious one? The timid one? The outgoing one? The brainiac? The longer we wear the mask we create, the more our behaviors morph into other damaging behaviors. The process is exhausting and uncomfortable.

The mask can be anything we promote about ourselves, such as a lifestyle of spending and social standing that conveys financial worth, success at work, or awards we earn. The world teaches us to spend more, hide more, be more. If you can achieve, it promises, you can become! Your mask could be makeup, hair and fashion: you display beauty to the world but crumble inside because no matter how much you cover and dress yourself up, you feel worthless and hollow.

The fashion industry pours millions of dollars each year into fine coverings. Each stitch, button, and hem is carefully constructed to frame our bodies. I highly appreciate the garment industry for its creative expression. There is a particular confidence one feels wearing a well-tailored outfit, accessorized with the perfect earrings, necklace, and bracelets. I loved fashion magazines and fashion TV shows growing up. I would look at the women and wonder what kind of lives they led. I would imagine how wonderful it would be to dress up all the time, to go out and be seen, and to have people adore you for how you looked. I would fantasize about how these fashionable women had superior confidence and how they could triumph over anything that came their way. They lived in big, fancy houses, had elaborate parties, and their men probably adored them. These fantasies led me to believe if I could somehow achieve that model look, the man, the house, and the car would come along with it. My prince charming would come to sweep me away in a luxury car, and we would live happily ever after.

Clothes can do a lot to enhance our figures, minimize our flaws and express our inner selves. For me, choosing clothing has always been fun. When I was a small child, I would stand in awe in my mother's closet and find the perfect outfit to dress up in. I always favored my mother's lingerie and high heels. Looking back now, it's hard for me to believe I was attracted to it, but I have fond memories of mom's silk gowns and lacy undergarments.

My love of dressing up continued into my adult life. Shopping became a means to feel a temporary high. I found clothes that made me feel sexy, smart, attractive, provocative, winsome, superior, polished, or put together. High heels gave me a sense of superiority. They made me taller and imparted feelings of being poised, sexy, and powerful. I'd say most women who wear heels probably feel the same way. There's something about adding a few inches of height that pumps up our confidence. However, if you wear heels any amount of time, you'll notice your toes being pushed together, squeezed like they're in some type of vise grip, or maybe the balls of your feet start to burn because the nerves in that part of the foot were never designed to bear that much weight. Even though these adornments are fashionable and good for confidence, they can be scary for the health of your feet.

In my attempts to feel better about myself, I estimate I had 30 pairs of high heels, one for every outfit, color, style, and design. These beautiful yet uncomfortable icons were damaging the nerves in my feet. I've witnessed the distorting effect heels can have on older women who develop bunions and misshapen bone growths. I'm not knocking high heels: I still find them attractive, and I have begun wearing them again. But my identity isn't tied to what they can do for me.

Maybe it's not heels for you. But you probably have some fig leaf for covering. Perhaps it takes the form of one of the following:

1. Busyness (you jump from one thing to another because if you rest and settle yourself, toxic, negative self-chatter takes over);
2. Being a workaholic (you work to feel important and needed);
3. Acting like a social butterfly (being around others to distract from your inner world);
4. Isolating yourself (using a room or home to hide behind);
5. Addiction (the use of drugs, alcohol, food, and relationships to numb feelings);
6. Religious activity (attending church and serving the Lord but not knowing Jesus personally).

Take an honest inventory right where you are. There is no shame in being honest with yourself. There is liberty in honesty and confession. Right where you are, if any of those apply to you, invite the Lord into your heart to remove the faulty fig leaves and let Him wrap and envelop you in His loving grace.

Pray: "Father, forgive me for using things of this world as a substitute for the real thing. I want to know You personally and intimately and I am going to let You know me personally and intimately. I want to see who You really are. Lift the veil of deception that has had me believe other things are life. But there's no ful-fillment in them. By faith, I believe You are life. Come lead me in Your life of abundant joy forevermore. Come open my heart and my eyes so that I can see the beauty of a relation-ship with You."

Pause and let Him speak to you.

Chapter 11—

REMADE A NEW CREATION

Now, if anyone is enfolded into Christ, he has become an entirely new person. All that is related to the old order has vanished. Behold, everything is fresh and new. And God has made all things new, and reconciled us to himself, and given us the ministry of reconciling others to God. In other words, it was through the Anointed One that God was shepherding the world, not even keeping records of their transgressions, and he has entrusted to us the ministry of opening the door of reconciliation to God. We are ambassadors of the Anointed

> One who carry the message of Christ to the
> world, as though God were tenderly pleading
> with them directly through our lips. So we ten-
> derly plead with you on Christ's behalf, "Turn
> back to God and be reconciled to him." For
> God made the only one who did not know sin
> to become sin for us, so that we might become
> the righteousness of God through our union
> with him.
> (2 Corinthians 5:17–21, TPT)

Jesus went to Calvary, purchased our salvation, and made it possible for us to become a new creation through Him. When we join our lives with Christ by receiving what He did on the cross for us, by faith, our lives are united and hidden in Him. God no longer sees our sinful nature. He sees Christ's reflection. By His mercy, we are made new. God looks down upon you with loving grace because He sees you as He sees His Son: you are now His son/daughter, with whom He is well pleased.

We don't work for salvation; we work from salvation because we have been justified through faith. Through His blood and faith, we have the right to be His heirs and to receive new life. It is through this Word that we become alive in Him.

Grasping His great love makes us want to serve Him and others. Knowing we will never be good enough to accomplish salvation on our own, this reality releases a deep level of worship because how could we ever have a new and different life without Him? Hallelujah!

Walking out Sanctification

Justification is free, but sanctification comes with a cost. This process of stripping off the old and taking on the new requires action on your part. It requires personal intimacy with the Lord, such as through getting in solitude with scripture and asking the Holy Spirit to speak to you through His Word and make you new.

In the Old Testament, physical circumcision was symbolic of being one of God's holy and set apart people. In the New Testament, circumcision is spiritual. It signifies removing the stony and rebellious heart and replacing it with a heart of flesh (Ezekiel 36:26). A stony, rebellious heart insists on living apart from the teachings of Christ and guidance of the Holy Spirit. A heart of flesh is alive unto Christ by the guidance and leading of the Holy Spirit. On our own, we don't have power over old mindsets, habits, beliefs, sins, iniquities, and transgressions. Only Christ can renew our minds and how we live life, and He will only do so with our permission. Our permission comes with our yes when we receive the truths from God's written Word.

We receive the kingdom in seed form. This means you can receive Christ and remain with only a kernel of the kingdom. If you never read another word in the Bible, your faith only functions in a small, hard and nearly lifeless form. But if you take the Word of God and allow it to water the seed, then your seed will grow and flourish. Actively reading and studying His Word provides power for transformation. The living water softens this seed, makes it take root in our heart, allows it to grow, and it then ripens and brings forth fruit in time. This fruit is the evidence of the righteousness of Christ in you.

Renewing Your Mind

The apostle Paul wrote, "Do not conform to the pattern of this world, but be transformed by the renewing of your mind. Then you will be able to test and approve what God's will is—his good, pleasing and perfect will" (Romans 12:2, NIV). His Word is miraculous, and reading it transforms what you think. You begin to see yourself and what you do in the light of His Word.

The Bible reads you as much as you read it. It knows your ways and will highlight what the Lord wants to deal with, one step at a time. Through grace, the power of His Holy Spirit works within you to deal with sin and allow you to walk in God's light. We serve a gracious God. He knows we are a shambled mess. That's why He sent His Son to do it all for us: year after year of offering sacrifices could never make us holy. What we do sacrificially will never make us holy; it is only by His power within us, through consistent reading of the Word, that we can be made new and exemplify holiness in our thoughts, beliefs and actions.

We must renew our minds. What is born of faith is generated from the heart. The mind, though, by reason or logic, will often cancel what we're called to do by faith. However, with renewed minds, we can know God's will for our lives and enter the flow of what Christ wants to accomplish.

An unrenewed mind rebels against the flow of faith every time. The soul is filled with moral filth, idolatry, impulses and needs of its own. What do you think about on most days? If you reflect on the question honestly, you'll probably find many of your thoughts are pretty repulsive. Most are born from selfishness, greed, envy, lust, or jealousy. They are self-gratify-ing—whatever pleases your senses is what you choose. They could be filled with pride, arrogance, self-pity, doubt, depression, or anxiety. There are a whole host of things your thoughts are full of that aren't part of the kingdom of God.

The fruits of the Holy Spirit outflow from a transformed mind: love, joy, peace, forbearance, kindness, goodness, faithfulness, gentleness, and self-control. (Galatians 5:22–23) A mind set on the things of the spirit is different than a mind set on the flesh that says, *NOW! I cannot wait.* It's impulsive. It demands its way.

Perhaps you're thinking, *This is a lot to take in. This is too much work.*

It is work, but thankfully we serve a gracious Father that gives us strengthening in our times of need to help us overcome. By grace working through you, being obedient will be possible.

The Fear of the Lord is a healthy attitude. This fear is not generated from a cowering position but from one of awe and wonder. It's the desire to not grieve God who has bought back your life from the grave. He does the heavy work when we lay down and surrender whatever He wishes us to.

As we go to the gym to work on physical fitness, we begin with lighter weights. As we build muscle, we can lift heavier and heavier weights. But going up in weight never comes without a cost. There is soreness, required rest time for recovery, and we'll need plenty of hydration and proper nourishment. Hydration is like the flow of the Spirit, and nourishment is like the Word of God. As we grow and mature in faith, it is done through Him, not on our own. We must be ingrafted into the true vine (John 15:4). We must stay planted by His rivers to flourish (Psalm 1:3).

I never said it was easy; I just said it was possible! Jesus said, "Whoever wants to save their life will lose it, but whoever loses their life for me will find it" (Matthew 16:25, NIV). Wow! Those are powerful words. You can keep doing what you are doing and satisfy your own pleasures constantly, stay in your comfort zone, and never receive the fullness of the spirit of grace. Or you can say, "Jesus, I see in Your Word this is what You want out of me. Help me. Change me. I'm willing!"

And as you feel His leading, follow Him.

Chapter 12—

THE LORD'S CALLING

And they heard the sound of the LORD God walking in the garden in the cool [afternoon breeze] of the day, so the man and his wife hid and kept themselves hidden from the presence of the Lord God among the trees of the garden. But the Lord God called to Adam, and said to him, "Where are you?" (Genesis 3:8–9, AMP)

A s God went looking for Eve and Adam, God comes looking for us!

Our God is omnipresent, which means He is everywhere at once. He is omniscient, which means He knows all things. He is omnipotent—in control of all things. So, why would God ask Adam where he was?

God invites us to a relationship, not to submit to a dictatorship. He wants confession and accountability. When He asks Adam, "Where are you?", He wants Adam to disclose his actions and tell what he's done.

> **Confess your sins to each other and pray for each other so that you may be healed. The earnest prayer of a righteous person has great power and produces wonderful results.**
> **(James 5:16, NLT)**

Since God knows us, He doesn't have to condemn us of sin; He already knows our weaknesses. He addresses sin in our lives because it causes disruption in our souls. It creates barriers to intimacy with Him, ourselves, and others. It causes shame, which leads to hiding, masking, and playing out behaviors far from our identity in Christ.

Notice how He creates a safe place of love where grace makes room for mistakes. Accountability restores our connection to the Father. There are consequences for our behavior, but we are never cut off from God's love. If God wanted to control the circumstances for Adam and Eve, He would have never allowed them to eat the forbidden fruit from the tree. He certainly would go to them immediately afterward to review their sin. He could have screamed, "Why would you do this to Me? Why? I told you it would kill you!" He could have continued on a diatribe of disappointment for hours, even days! But He didn't.

He calmly asked where they were because He wanted them to respond from relationship.

Adam replied: "I heard the sound of You [walking] in the garden, and I was afraid because I was naked; so I hid myself" (Genesis 3:10, AMP).

He saw himself as naked, vulnerable, and ashamed. Why would disobedience bring him shame? Why was he ashamed of the perfect body God had designed? Because sin inevitably makes us feel shame. When we feel shame, we hide and try to mask all that we feel when we disobey God.

In their actions, Adam and Eve reveal how most of us respond when God comes looking for us in our guilt and shame. The Bible says He constantly pursues us. He continues going after us because of His great love for us.

You might be thinking, I don't hide: I'm just going about my life. I'm just having fun and doing what makes me happy. Happiness is a key to the soul being satisfied and happiness is good for you, but a life based around being happy isn't always the best qualifier for a good life.

Consider some questions:

— Does happiness keep you peaceful?
— Is happiness sustainable all the time?
— Does happiness comfort you in trials?

If you found those questions difficult to answer yes to, it's because happiness, even though wonderful, can't be sustained all the time.

I mention happiness because the world puts such a high value on this situational emotion. Happiness means you have to have something happening. But joy comes from the inside and through intimate communion with God.

Sustaining happiness all the time is impossible because we live in a fallen world. Seeking after happiness is like moving from one fig leaf to the other, one relationship to the next, one addiction to the next, one mall to the next store, one house to the next, and one town to another. If something doesn't work out, there is always another option. It never ends. The writer of Ecclesiastes puts it perfectly: it's all meaningless toil to get and to amass great pleasure, great wisdom, great wealth. It's all chasing after the wind because in the end, it has no meaning, and in the end, you lose your soul. It only stores up treasure for us here on earth, which will fade away when we do (Ecclesiastes 2).

So what am I recommending? Is God a fun stealer? NO! He is the absolute opposite. There is a place full of abundance but only in God. There is life that overflows. There is a place where joy, peace, love, and contentment exist to completely form to overflowing in someone. This is life abundant!

I came that they may have life and have it abundantly. (John 10:10, ESV)

— What is "life abundantly?"
— How do we get this kind of peace?
— How do we get this kind of comfort?
— How do we get this kind of joy?
— How do we get this kind of satisfaction?

The answer is RELATIONSHIP! Relationship with God, His Son Jesus and the Holy Spirit, which was His gift at the cross for us.

> **God said, "Who told you that you were naked? Have you eaten [fruit] from the tree of which I commanded you not to eat?"**
> **(Genesis 3:11, AMP)**

Since God knew what they did, why would He ask them for clarification? He wanted them to confess and repent. God still wants us to live clear and clean with a cleansed conscience. A cleansed conscience comes from confession and being honest with oneself and God. God can manage the rest: He just wants a heart that can admit wrong, one that says, "I confess that I have sinned against You, Father." There is no right or wrong way to go about it other than being completely honest with yourself and Him. He wants a relationship that is unbroken and fully alive. He wanted it with Adam and Eve, and He still wants it today. Any good father wants such a relationship with his child.

He identified the shame they felt, the nakedness, and the sin of disobedience.

Today He might ask: "Daughter, why do you seek identity from that group? Why do you chase after men who never give you the validation you're looking for? Why do you spend so much time trying to impress others? Why are you running from life? Who told you you weren't lovely? Who told you you were too much or too little? Who told you you couldn't make it? Who told you you would always be this way? Who told you why even try? Who told you that you couldn't?"

There are a million questions God has for us when we hide. He asks questions to offer an entry back into relationship. The best thing for us is the one thing He wants for us and with us. He wants us to feel the righteousness (right standing) His Son died to purchase for us. He wants us to have the power to overcome sin in our lives so we do not feel guilt or shame. And when we receive His Holy Spirit, His overcoming power is inside of us.

When we place our faith in Jesus, we are born again. The Holy Spirit is born within us. You receive the same spirit that literally raised Christ from the dead! This means when you receive Christ's finished work on the cross, by faith, you step into a realm of resurrection! A supernatural exchange happens when you receive Christ as Lord of your life, even though no popping bottle is heard or confetti thrown. However, in Heaven, it's quite different. I'm sure the angels ring bells and celebrate your faith and eternal life.

As I mentioned earlier, when I received Christ back into my life that evening on a cold, white tile floor, I felt hope for the first time in a long time. That, to me, was *life*. Life without hope is no life at all: it's all meaningless, whatever you do, because it doesn't lead to anything fruitful or abundant. Even though my circumstances had not changed, I had. The power that touched me was the power of being born again. It lit something within me to get up and fight for life. The chains of darkness fell when I was touched in that way because hell cannot prevail over the power of the blood from the cross.

When we are born again, we are promised the seal of the Holy Spirit. This seal signifies one's authorization as God's child. You are His. He is yours. The Father is so patient and so kind, it is by His long-suffering that none of us should perish. His love is also fierce and jealous, so when we do come to Him, His power within us gives a hope that we cannot help but fight for life. This second chance at life that He gives, gives us the power to overcome.

I'm sure you've needed power to overcome struggles against your temptations. You know there is greater meaning and purpose for your life. If you are wondering, I promise you God's spirit is leading you to Him to show you the road you are to travel that will bring meaning, life, and purpose. We are all made with purpose and for a specific reason. No one was made without careful design and intent. God doesn't make junk. He makes us fearfully and wonderfully. He knows every hair on our head; He knows our coming and our going; He knows our thoughts from afar. He designed us specifically, and intentionally places us because He designed us to be light and life to those around us, building a community to help one another.

Chapter 13—

CLOTHED IN RIGHTEOUSNESS

**The LORD God made garments of skin for Adam
and his wife and clothed them.
(Genesis 3:21, NIV)**

I n God's compassion and mercy towards Adam and Eve,
He removed the prickly sets of leaves they had made to
cover themselves and replaced them with animal hides.
The new covering showed the two-fold payment required for
sin atonement. One, an animal had to be sacrificed as a sin
offering, and two, its skin was used as a covering to protect
them from the new environment they would be placed in. The
act foreshadowed what was to come with atonement through

Christ. He would be the perfect Lamb slain for a one-time sacrifice for sin, and His body and blood would become the perfect righteousness to clothe us when we receive His work on the cross. The restoration was two-fold: it forgave us our sin and restored our closeness to the Father so that we could once again be covered in the glory of His love. We now enter into the Father's presence unashamed and unafraid because we are confident in the grace and mercy of our Lord Jesus Christ (Hebrews 4:16). This picture perfectly illustrates how God's faithfulness is one of justice and mercy. His love hangs in this beautiful balance.

"Therefore, if anyone cleanses himself from these things, he will be a vessel for honor, sanctified, useful to the Master, prepared for every good work" (2 Timothy 2:21, NASB1995). For the reason of glory, scripture says He chastens (disciplines) those He loves. Discipline here refers to instruction, correction, chastisement or rebuke; it doesn't mean condemnation or physical punishment. He has firm orders, boundaries, and headship to protect our souls and our hearts. We are led into a cleansing and purging process of our sin to become filled with Jesus, the hope of our glory.

> I will greatly rejoice in the Lord;
> my soul shall exult in my God,
> for he has clothed me with the garments of salvation;
> he has covered me with the robe of righteousness,
> as a bridegroom decks himself like a priest with
>   a beautiful headdress,

and as a bride adorns herself with her jewels.
(Isaiah 61:10, ESV)

He removes the uncomfortable masks and garments of protection that we have uncomfortably robed ourselves in and replaces them with the finest fabrics constructed to clothe a royal heir. He doesn't put us in just any clothes because we are now kings and priests unto Him. Jesus died to give us a royal standing—one with power, authority, and dominion in Him. When we receive Him, we receive His righteousness. We receive nothing of our own doing because, in our flesh, we could never do what needs to be done to create this right standing. Only through His sacrifice do we receive this kind of extravagance.

So what does this actually look like?

I am my beloved's and my beloved is mine;
he browses among the lilies.
(Song of Songs 6:3, NIV)

There is a place of quiet surrender inside that rests in the salvation of Jesus. He is my reward, my joy, my peace. I no longer have to worry about my salvation or whether I am good enough or pleasing enough. The questions have been answered, and I am fully persuaded and confident that I am fully loved. I am perfectly His and He is perfectly mine. The fellowship with Jesus and His Holy Spirit dwelling within me provides a constant, fluid awareness of my connection with the Lord.

For me, taking off fear looked like putting on trust.

> The LORD is my rock and my fortress and my
>   deliverer,
> my God, my rock, in whom I take refuge,
> my shield, and the horn of my salvation,
> my stronghold and my refuge,
> my savior; you save me from violence.
> I call upon the Lord, who is worthy to be praised,
> and I am saved from my enemies.
> (2 Samuel 22:2–4, ESV)

Trusting in the Lord has given me confidence instead of anxiety. I have built a history with the Lord to know His goodness is certain. When I have called out to Him, He has been faithful to rescue and restore me. I use that confidence in the next battle, the next hardship, the next assignment that requires faith. I can stand with confidence because God is true to His Word, and He will not fail me.

Taking off shame looked like putting on honor.

> At that time I will deal
> with all who oppressed you.
> I will rescue the lame;
> I will gather the exiles.
> I will give them praise and honor
> in every land where they have suffered shame.
> (Zephaniah 3:19, NIV)

Being able to write this book has been a beautiful testimony of reversing shame for honor. I am honored to share the battles the Lord has helped me overcome. I am not ashamed of my past before I met the mercy of the Lord.

Taking off promiscuity looked like putting on covenant love.

I am jealous for you with a jealousy that comes from God. I promised to give you to Christ. He must be your only husband. I want to give you to Christ to be his pure bride. But I am afraid that your minds will be led away from the true and pure following of Christ. This could happen just as Eve was tricked by that snake with his clever lies. (2 Corinthians 11:2-3 ERV)

I laid down all other lovers for my One Thing, King Jesus. Promiscuity for me wasn't just with other men, it was with other lovers as well: material wealth, power, control, prestige. Now I love chasing after the things of God. The chase is the most thrilling part of living in Christ. He speaks to me and gives me a word. He gives me a dream or vision that I can cling to and research because I know He wants to reveal a deeper facet of His love toward me.

Taking off cigarettes looked like inhaling His ruach breath.

The Spirit of God has made me,
and the breath of the Almighty gives me life.
(Job 33:4, NIV)

Frustration used to lead me to smoking a cigarette. Now I just breathe. I know the Spirit of God is within that breath and wants me to exchange my anxious, spiraling thoughts for wisdom to encounter the situation affecting my emotions. He is always faithful to fill me with just what I need to get through challenging moments.

Taking off alcohol and looked like drinking the new wine of His Spirit.

> Do not get drunk on wine, which leads to debauchery. Instead, be filled with the Spirit, speaking to one another with psalms, hymns, and songs from the Spirit. Sing and make music from your heart to the Lord.
> (Ephesians 5:18–19, NIV)

Wine used to fill every portion of my thoughts, my imaginations and desires. It determined where I would eat dinner, whose house I would visit, if I would go out at night, who I would surround myself with. It was an all-consuming desire. When I was delivered of the spirit of addiction, wine was no longer a desire—only the consuming fire of knowing what the Lord revealed to me. I am addicted to the Lord!

Removing barrenness looked like putting on fruitfulness.

> This is what the Sovereign Lord says: On the day I cleanse you from all your sins, I will resettle your towns, and the ruins will be

rebuilt. The desolate land will be cultivated instead of lying desolate in the sight of all who pass through it. They will say, "This land that was laid waste has become like the garden of Eden; the cities that were lying in ruins, desolate and destroyed, are now fortified and inhabited."
(Ezekiel 36:33–35, NIV)

What was once a barren wasteland of negative thinking and negative behaviors is now fruitful with the fruits of the Spirit, love, joy, peace, patience, faithfulness, gentleness, kindness and self-control. My life bears the fruit of walking with the Lord and listening closely to His tender directions. Choosing a marriage partner, deciding to have children, and opening my business were all choices that I clearly discerned through time spent in prayer with the Lord.

Taking off rejection looked like putting on belonging.

You did not choose me, but I chose you and appointed you so that you might go and bear fruit—fruit that will last—and so that whatever you ask in my name the Father will give you. This is my command: Love each other.
(John 15:16–17, NIV)

The revelation that God chose me first was mind blowing. I thought it was somehow my awakening responsibility to come to my senses and reach out to Him. That thinking was clearly off base, for God chose me first and wooed me in with His sovereign love. He closed every other door of seeking satisfaction in this world so that I could fix my eyes on Jesus and become the woman He designed me to be.

He is now speaking a better Word over your life right now: love, joy, peace and healing. So, step into this grace that loved you before you loved Him!

Taking off fear of failure looked like putting on bravery and courage.

> Have I not commanded you? Be strong and courageous. Do not be afraid; do not be discouraged, for the LORD your God will be with you wherever you go.
> (Joshua 1:9, NIV)

He encourages us to put off our negative, doubtful, distrusting, evil (unbelieving and hardened hearts) and carnal (worldly) mindsets. The apostle Paul wrote: "Whatever things are true, whatever things are noble, whatever things are just, whatever things are pure, whatever things are lovely, whatever things are of good report, if there is any virtue and if there is anything praiseworthy—meditate on these things" (Philippians 4:8 NKVJ).

The Lord reroutes our desires so that they become ones that are purified by His Word. He takes the emotions of our hearts, sanctifies them and turns what now grieves us into what grieves Him. The veil lifts to see what is really important in this lifetime that impacts eternity. It's the God thing over the good thing. He takes our brokenness and makes it beautiful, the artful tapestry of His grace interwoven into our stories. His grace is limitless, and His mercies never cease (Lamentations 3:22–23). Will you step into His love?

CONCLUSION

Today my life looks very different than it did in 2013 when I began my metamorphosis with Christ. It has not been an easy journey but one worth the pain, tears and sacrifice. There were many times I was tempted to run back to my old behaviors and mindsets, but the Lord was there to meet me through scripture, the encouragement of a friend, a message while scrolling on Facebook or Instagram. A quick glance would reveal a nugget of biblical truth and enable me to refocus my efforts: I could be confident a life in Christ was possible and breakthroughs were on the way.

I have now been married seven years to my husband Bill and we have two beautiful children. The perseverance and endurance I developed during my time of recovery have been instrumental in the challenges and trials of marriage and family. Knowing how to run to the Father when trials and tribulations run amuck in life has been invaluable. No one knows you like God does and no one has the perfect advice for a problem like the Lord. He has led and guided me through His Word and through inner wisdom to seek wise counsel when problems were too much to sort through on my own.

The biggest takeaway I hope you receive is that a relationship with Jesus is the most important relationship to invest your life in. He will never leave nor forsake you. He is there in the fires and floods of life. He gives joy when happiness cannot be found, and He gives strength when you are weary. He gives courage for fear. He gives light for the next step. I am confident that if it hadn't been for Christ in my life, I would not be where I am now. All praise to King Jesus!

ACKNOWLEDGMENTS

T hank you to Laura Thompson for proofreading. Thank you to Rachel Hall, of Writely Divided Editing and More, for line and copy editing, proofreading and manuscript formatting.

ABOUT THE AUTHOR

T his is the first book written by Elizabeth Clements. She and her husband Bill reside in Salisbury, NC, with their two children, daughter, Annelise and son, Ellison. Elizabeth owns and operates Hairapy by Elizabeth, a hair studio salon in downtown Salisbury. As a full-time hairstylist, she uses her artistic craft as an opportunity to engage clients on a deep, personal level and point them to the love of Jesus.

When she's not behind the chair, she enjoys spending time with her family, reading, cooking, and being out in nature.

Elizabeth was born again in 2013 through a powerful encounter with Jesus that changed her whole trajectory of life. In this new love affair with the Lord, He called her out of a life of addiction, pain and inner turmoil. As Christ renewed her mind, body and spirit, she developed a longing to see the transformation of others. Elizabeth is passionate about growing in her gifting and high calling in Christ, helping equip others in the faith, and in strengthening the body of Christ at large to prepare for our Lord's coming again.

Elizabeth says: "I long to see others transformed by the power and presence of Jesus Christ. It is my mission to make Jesus famous for all He has done."

A free ebook edition is available with the purchase of this book.

To claim your free ebook edition:

1. Visit MorganJamesBOGO.com
2. Sign your name CLEARLY in the space
3. Complete the form and submit a photo of the entire copyright page
4. You or your friend can download the ebook to your preferred device

Morgan James
BOGO™

A **FREE** ebook edition is available for you or a friend with the purchase of this print book.

CLEARLY SIGN YOUR NAME ABOVE

Instructions to claim your free ebook edition:
1. Visit MorganJamesBOGO.com
2. Sign your name CLEARLY in the space above
3. Complete the form and submit a photo of this entire page
4. You or your friend can download the ebook to your preferred device

Print & Digital Together Forever.

Snap a photo

Free ebook

Read anywhere